THE PATH HOME

A Perspective to Discovering Joy

By Patrick McKeon

THE PATH HOME

ACKNOWLEDGEMENTS & GRATITUDE

First, for Greg Amundson. We haven't met in person, at least not yet, but I could not have asked for a more gracious, patient and supportive mentor as an author, especially as a first-time author. You embody the very best of humanity and the human spirit. I am forever grateful for your time.

For Mom and my brother Justin. To summarize a lifetime of gratitude in a sentence is a humbling exercise. We learned, grew, cried, fought and loved...together. Thank you for being the models of perseverance I so often sought to exemplify. Your hearts are more immense and caring than you realize.

For my children: Jack, Cate, Hank and Elle. I absolutely love being your Dad. It is a privilege I cherish on a daily basis. Seeing how you shine your light is an endless example of how I seek to live my own life. Continue to do so, as you are meant for a wonderful journey in this world. I humbly look forward to serving as a guide on your path, just as you are in mine. Please know in your heart that today, and all days into perpetuity, I love being your Dad.

Lastly, and most profoundly, for Cathy. Thank you for your smile. For walking down this path with me starting one summer all those years ago. For your free spirit and sense of adventure. For your steadfast belief that anything is possible, no matter how wild it may seem. For being the rock of strength and grace on which our family is built. Our time walking the path of life together always feels like it's just beginning. Always.

ABOUT THE BOOK

Before we venture into who this book is for and even a summary of the story itself, allow me to provide insight on how, and why, our story reads a particular way. As I read, whether a book, a magazine or even our children's composition homework, I visualize the story coming to life in my mind's eye. Essentially, I am creating a movie out of the litany of words on the paper (or screen) in front of me. This may be something you do as well, or it may not. I only offer that as a pattern of how I absorb written content with no consideration to a "right" or "wrong" way.

However, this does help clarify why when time came for me to perform the act of writing a story, I found myself subconsciously drifting in the same direction. Which is to say I envisioned the events of *The Path Home* in my mind's eye. As such, our narrator was tasked with the intention of transforming that vision into written word. The result of that exercise is that you may find this story reads more like a movie or a play, instead of a traditional book.

Regardless of how you consume the words in the pages that follow, be it visually or otherwise, I am left with only one wish for you: I hope you enjoy the show.

WHO IS THIS BOOK FOR?

Optimistically, this story is for a wide audience, so wide, in fact, that it's hard to name the full contingent. I guess that's every author's dream scenario, isn't it?

Having said that, though, it is with a profound sense of gratitude that I thank *you* for taking the time to read *The Path Home*. I have absolute faith that this book has found you in the right place on your own path, whether it be in the unfolding of a new chapter of life or at a crossroad lying in front of you. This book is for you, in this moment.

May this story provide perspective on how life happens *for* us and not to us. I do understand my limitations to fully appreciate or know whatever it is that has happened in your life, be it painful, glorious, tragic or magical, that brought this story into your hands at this time. However, I do believe that if we search hard enough, and dig deep enough, that we can find some semblance of good in all we experience. For where there is good, there are light and love. While walking the path towards this truth may not be easy, in fact quite likely the opposite, these are always steps worth taking. For what you find on this trail may be something you are searching for, perhaps what we are all searching for...*The Path Home*.

In all sincerity, from a personal perspective, the ideal audience for this story is my children. They don't inspire the book per se; they inspire the author. If they are the only four people in the world that read it, then it was time well spent. If they take from it something that helps them understand our relationship and why I speak or act the way I do as their Dad, then it's an honor to give them that gift. And if by any chance it provides them a glimpse into my soul and some water for the seed of purpose that was planted in theirs, then I know the world will be a better place as that seed continues to grow and flourish.

As time passes, I hope this story will be one part of how I intentionally continue to live into the promise that I made to myself a long time ago to be a "great dad". Not in my eyes, but in theirs.

SUMMARY OF THE PATH HOME

Life truly is a journey full of twists, turns and interesting characters. It's that way for all of us. *The Path Home* opens the door to my story and several truths I've discovered (and perhaps in some cases, rediscovered) as the seasons of time unfolded.

No person's life is perfect, and our paths are rarely straight and narrow. However, there are lessons woven throughout every single one of our experiences. In this book, there are several moments that define a life, my life, or so I thought. In some respects, the review of my own experiences makes this book autobiographical in nature. While the signature events of the book did in fact occur as part of my own path, details and participants are reimagined for purposes of providing you, the reader, with the ability to fully engage in the underlying truths. Perhaps, how *you* may engage those truths in your own life supersede how they occurred in mine.

This story takes place in Bayonne, New Jersey. If you haven't heard of it, that's fine. No judgement here. Simply think of every story, movie or song you know about New Jersey, and Bayonne embodies them all: gritty and blue-collar to its core, but with a depth of humanity that is largely misunderstood. Like its people, the city's connections run far deeper and broader than any external image or reputation may imply. In short, Bayonne is Jersey, in all her splendid, and sometimes sordid, glory.

If you have heard of it, wonderful! That means we're probably either related somehow or your aunt worked with my mom, and both of us graduated from the same preschool. Or maybe your grandmother knew my grandmother from the bingo club, and both of them were one of twelve children. You know how wild and wacky a family tree can really get. Either way, now you know another person from Bayonne. And once you get to know someone from the Golden Peninsula, they're family. That's just the way it works, in all its splendid, and sometimes sordid, glory.

As mentioned, *The Path Home* is a reflection on my life and several of the events that shaped my own path. However, rather than simply recount stories of life's challenges and how I reacted in the moment, I chose to implement a different take on life's various crucibles. Instead, I examined those moments with a deeper perspective and how those moments shaped not only my life, but those of many, with rippling connections well beyond my scope of understanding. Candidly, in its most essential form, *The Path Home* is a search to find the good in all we experience.

Through that exploration, I've come to truly believe that the impact we have on each other and those around us is far more expansive than we appreciate, even for those we hardly know at all, or think we know, anyway. Perhaps you will realize, as I did, that our life's journey never really ends insomuch as it continues on in the lives and tales of others, weaving wisdom and connection through the passage of time.

Ultimately, then, what can we all discover, what truths lie hidden in plain sight, if we examine our lives with a different lens and an open heart? The events of the past might not look any different, but how would today and each day thereafter look? After all, the gift of those truths is not meant for our sole benefit, but rather to serve as a gift for those we love.

TABLE OF CONTENTS

SECTION ONE:
THE DAY EVERYTHING CHANGED

SECTION TWO:
ONE STEP BACK, TWO STEPS FORWARD?

SECTION THREE:
THE WALL BETWEEN

SECTION FOUR:
CRACKING THE COCONUT

SECTION FIVE:
GRACE COMES HOME

SECTION ONE

The Day Everything Changed

A Sunny Tuesday Morning

1

THE MAJESTIC SKYLINE OF LOWER MANHATTAN IN SEPTEMBER 2001. LINED WITH SOARING CASTLES OF STEEL AND GLASS, HOME TO THOUSANDS UPON THOUSANDS OF INDIVIDUALS SEEKING TO CARVE THEIR PATH WITHIN THE GRAND MANIFESTATION OF COMMERCE AND TRADE IN THE 21ST CENTURY.

The Twin Towers standing in the center of it all, resolute pillars exemplifying the belief that we can live amidst the sky. Two powerful chambers serving as the beating heart of New York City. Their inhabitants skimming the clouds of possibility each and every day.

A picture-perfect Tuesday morning, the 11th of September. Temperature in the low sixties, a slight breeze blowing in off the Hudson River. The sky glimmering a pristine shade of powder blue.

It's days like these that make working in an office so painful. Why in the world would anyone want to be cooped up inside on a day like today? Everyone has a laptop nowadays; would it be so odd to conduct a meeting and send emails from outside? These are philosophical musings and minor frustrations in Jimmy's day.

Such is life when you're floating on Cloud Nine.

Twenty-two years old, Jimmy is nearly a year into working for a Big Five accounting firm auditing financial service companies. Think banks and brokerage firms. Confidently striding into another day at the office with everything he planned in life coming to fruition. Only better than he previously imagined.

Jimmy and Quinn are officially dating now. A few years of friendship and courtship evolved into an enchanting romance. Despite a thousand miles between them, Quinn is now an undergraduate student at the University of Florida. Jimmy knows it's only the beginning of something truly special. Every time they are together, he feels like it's the beginning of a great adventure.

He skipped out on Monday Night Football beers and wings with his audit team. Always preferring to watch the Giants (his Giants) from the comforts of home with his brother Bryan. Plus, he made plans to fly down to Florida and visit Quinn in a few days. Earlier than he anticipated for his first visit of the school year, but she secured two tickets to the Florida/Tennessee football game this coming Saturday. With seats in the student section ten rows up from the field no less. He has to make that trip!

A hastily executed last-minute decision and, unfortunately, he booked his flight before asking his managers. Fingers crossed when he mentions it later this morning, they will approve his request for Friday off. The timing is terrible, as this week they are kicking off one of the largest engagements in their division, and now isn't exactly the best time to ask for a few days of sunshine and football, even if it is just a long weekend.

Luckily, his bosses are both huge college football fans. He knows they will understand, albeit with baited-breath. Approval will come with conditions, though, and he is prepared to graciously accept any terms. A few all-nighters in the office in order to see Quinn? Easy trade. Easy.

The audit client is an international investment bank head-quartered in One World Financial Center. Their host kindly set up the team with a conference room on the 33rd Floor. One World Financial (colloquially shortened to World Fi) is part of the overall World Trade Center complex. This office building, in particular, is located directly across the street from the Twin Towers on the marina side of West Street.

The energy of the entire complex is immense. The hustle and bustle of New York at its finest. And not just New York, but the entire financial world. Working in the maelstrom of high finance is a privilege, one that Jimmy views as earned. He appreciates every moment of it, soaking in all aspects as he settles into a career in the "working world".

His colleagues don't know it, not many people do, but the Twin Towers hold a devoutly special place in his heart. Growing up on the Jersey side of the Hudson, they served as the backdrop of every trip on the Jersey Turnpike to and from his hometown of Bayonne. The Towers were also there in high school, when he was a student at the Jesuit school in downtown Jersey City. They framed the background for team photos, awards ceremonies and championship baseball games. An ever-present reminder of the majesty and allure of the Big Apple.

Also, the location of his first unofficial "date" with Quinn a year ago. A dinner together at Windows on the World, the chic restaurant located on the 107th floor of the North Tower. They had no business being there, kids merely masquerading as adults. Jimmy with a poorly constructed necktie, Quinn giggling as each course of the meal was unveiled. But they were kids that didn't quite care what anyone else thought. Through the evening, as each new plate was brought to the table, they were falling in love with each other. Nothing else mattered, least of all the proper pronunciation of crème brûlée.

These thoughts, along with visions of the future together with Quinn, accompany Jimmy on each morning's commute on the PATH, the underground train connecting New Jersey to New York City. As a result, he often finds himself to be the happiest person on the train. Smiles, even faint ones, are odd sites in the packed commuter car.

Jimmy is exactly where he wants to be in the world and knows exactly where life is going next.

On this beautiful morning, finding himself carrying his smile all the way to his desk in the team's adopted home base, the internal conference room that will be their home away from home for the next six months. The bleak grayish blue painted conference room with decades old fluorescent lighting has no external windows, just a window pane with vertical blinds on one wall offering a glimpse of the operations floor. No matter. The view of the nearby Towers is part of him. Easily accessible whenever he wants.

Eager to get a jump on the day's work and show a commitment to his team, especially with his weekend plans pending, means arriving at the office first that day. Sitting down at his desk in the dimly lit far corner of the room facing his very own section of the grayish blue wall. Jimmy expected to receive the spot furthest away from the managers. A corporate hazing if you will. Exile the young guy to the corner to see if he can handle it. Ignoring the conditions of his outpost, he is excited to open his bulky laptop and kick off what he envisions will be another busy day of learning, planning and executing the complex engagement ahead of them.

His computer showing his start time for the day, a touch after 8:00 a.m. A quiet start to the day. Being alone helps that too. Easy to focus. Jimmy doesn't expect anyone else on the team to arrive until after 9:00 a.m. Plenty of time for him to get a jump on the day.

8:46 a.m.

BOOM! A deafening roar piercing the silent morning sky, coming to an abrupt end with a thunderous explosion. **BANG!** The office tower at One World Financial Center shaking as if the earth itself trembled. Desks and walls rattling. Coffee cups and picture frames falling over.

Startled, Jimmy's hands tense up, the muscles in his back and arms constrict, forcing his shoulders upwards towards his ears. "What the??" he says to himself. With no view of the outside, Jimmy has no idea what the sound could be.

"Holy shit!" someone from the Operations department shouts outside the office. The floor immediately up in arms. Everyone scrambling and shouting a different version of, "What the hell was that?" They all sound afraid. But of what?

Nearly everyone simultaneously picks up a desk phone.

Jimmy quickly warms to the idea of investigating a bit further. Walking over to the window adjacent the desk of one of the senior executives he only recently became close with. Even at just twenty-two years old and a year into his career as an auditor, Jimmy knows building trust and relationship are important. And the guy with the window seat is usually a good guy to become friends with.

Jimmy, peering out the window behind the large dark wooden desk, glancing upwards towards the sky. Blackness coming into view. A gaping hole. Tar-colored smoke billowing from the side of the North Tower of the World Trade Center. A crater replacing the steel and glass exterior. "What the??"

"Crazy shit, right kid?" the executive calmly stating. Not even remotely concerned at the moment. "Yeah, but what? A helicopter? Maybe a private jet that went off course?" Neither answer feels right. The executive simply shrugging, then grumbling,

"I guess we'll find out soon enough." His gaze remaining on the floor of people in front of him, not what lies behind.

Jimmy anxiously walks back to his desk, still the lone member of his team in the office, and calls Quinn. Figuring she will be starting her day right about now. Despite the inherent nature of their long-distance relationship, she's always the first person he thinks of.

"Morning, Q. Can you put on the news when you have a second? The Trade Center has been hit by something, what I don't know. I'm really not sure what happened yet. No one around here is."

On the other end of the line, the sound of searching for a remote and the click of the TV turning on. "My God. What is that?" Quinn in shock as the scene on TV unfolds. "Where are you? Do you have to get out of there?"

"I'm across the street, remember the World Fi buildings I showed you? I'm not sure what's going on. No one is leaving though. They told us to stay put, there's no need to evacuate. Seems like it's just a weird thing that happened. Pretty wild I'm here for it though."

"Yeah, but if it's not safe then you need to leave. Promise me that. It doesn't look good."

"I will. Promise."

After hanging up Jimmy walks back over to the window near the executive. The office still buzzing, and he is still a little too rattled to resume his work for the day. Maybe checking things out again will settle him down.

Back at the glass wall, glancing for a second time up at the void across the street. Smoke continuing to pour out. Above the impact zone, an image catches his eye. A man stands at the ledge of a window a few floors above the crater. Appearing to stare at the smoke below. Jimmy's thoughts quickly turning.

"Come on man, get out of there! GO! What are you waiting for?! GO. NOW!"

A moment later, the man jumps.

"Oh God, no." Jimmy's eyes lock in on the man from the moment the man decides to end his life. The step off the ledge. Following him through the air, smoke and debris until his final resting place hundreds of feet below on the roof of the Marriott Hotel.

His lifeless body lying contorted in a pool of blood.

Jimmy's stomach plummets. Instant nausea. Nearly vomiting on the spot. Managing to hold it in, but quickly racing back to the office. Quinn...calling her again. No answer. Again. No answer. He needs to tell someone what he just saw. However horrible. Was that even real? Is this happening right now?

His right leg shaking furiously as the receiver continues ringing. Nervously twisting and untwisting the phone cord tightly around his left hand as he waits for Quinn's voice in his right ear. No answer. What now?

9:03 a.m.

Overhead the same thunderous sound piercing the morning sky. Intense, powerful, roaring. **BOOM!** Another blast outside. The building shaking again. A second round of desk clutter falling to the floor.

Jimmy's body doesn't flinch; he now recognizes the ominous sound of a jet engine. "Attack" is the only word coming to mind. One word that changes everything.

"Everybody, get the hell out. NOW!" The executive with the window seat commanding everyone on the floor. "Everyone. NOW."

Jimmy picks up the phone, calling Quinn again. Wanting to tell her it is an attack, it's time to evacuate and would call when he was safe. The ringing again vibrating in the receiver,

"Come on, come on, answer. Please answer." Call her when he was safe? Is he sure he will be? No answer. Does he leave a message?

He hangs up the phone. Immediately picking up the receiver again, dialing her cell phone number...352...

"Kid! No time for phone calls. Get the hell out of here. NOW! We're all leaving, you included!" The executive paused at the office door to make sure Jimmy left with everyone. Committed to leaving no person behind.

One more shot...352...Damn. No answer. "Okay, I'm coming."

"Don't grab anything. Just GO!!" No time for a message. He'll call Quinn later.

No second alarm or announcement to evacuate the building ever comes. Everyone just knows what to do. Jimmy seamlessly weaves into the river of people marching down the darkened emergency exit stairway. After one flight of stairs, he notices how quiet it is, like sitting in Sunday church service. Of the thousands of people in the procession, no one speaks to one another. Thirty-two more flights down until the exit.

Everyone moving silently together, each person attempting to call loved ones from their cell phones. No call going through. The faint lime green light from the phone screens guides each step towards the exit. Jimmy is no different than anyone else. Quinn's cell phone number burning deeper and deeper into his memory with each failed attempt.

352...

The quiet strikes him for a moment. Amazed at how organized and calm everyone appears. Then it dawns on him.

No one in the stairway knows what is waiting for them on the other side of the exit. There are no windows. No view to the outside. No communications. Did another plane hit? Are there armed soldiers in the street? After all, this is an *attack*.

The possibilities race through his mind. Everyone's mind. Each person is scared to die. A picturesque Fall morning in lower Manhattan turning into a war zone. No one certain of the outcome.

The Way Home

2

STEEL EXIT DOORS SWINGING OPENING. LIGHT
FLOODING THE STAIRWAY. UPON BREACHING THE
THRESHOLD TO OUTSIDE, JIMMY SHIELDS HIS EYES
WITH HIS LEFT HAND IN ORDER TO SEE CLEARLY AND
GATHER HIS BEARINGS. LISTENING INTENTLY FOR ANY
OTHER THREATENING SOUNDS IN THE SKY ABOVE.

He quickly surveys the scene once outside. No other planes. No armed soldiers in the streets or immediate threats visible. Momentary relief. But now what?

The emergency exit empties to the marina side of the World Financial Center, situated between the Hudson River and the Twin Towers. Not an ideal location for figuring out where to go next. Flipping open his new silver cell phone, continuing to call Quinn, desperate to let her know he was safely out of the building. Still nothing. Phones lines are down. There would be no getting through any time soon.

Can he tell her he is safe though?

Squinting his eyes from the glare of the sun as he glances upwards towards the Towers. Debris. Smoke. And the most disturbing site of all: more people leaping to their death. Several times hurdling towards the ground hand in hand.

Something instantly awakes inside him. He needs *to move*. He *needs* to get home. Although home is in New Jersey, in Hoboken. On the other side of the river. No trains running. Tunnels closed. No bridges to cross. How then?

The ferry.

Glancing apprehensively to the other side of the marina, locating the ferry stop. Hoping beyond hope the boat is still there. *Yes!* It's at the dock! A stroke of good fortune. Thankfully the boat looks as though it's still loading passengers. There's only one problem, getting to the boat requires navigating the U-shaped marina. Which necessitates first walking closer to the Towers, then back out towards the ferry.

Jimmy thinks for a split second before taking his first step towards the burning buildings, "It's the only way home." He then begins the walk, oddly not a sprint nor even a jog, around the marina. There's no apparent need to rush, everyone else around him is walking as well. Even those bloodied and wounded by falling debris. The pace is strangely more akin to a mid-morning coffee break than a life-threatening terrorist attack.

A collective shock numbs the entire area. No one conceiving that the worst is yet to come.

The middle of the U-shaped path passes the entrance to the marina. It's there at the spot nearest to the Towers a person appears in the corner of Jimmy's right eye, immediately catching his attention. The man is standing alone. Simply standing calmly amidst the throngs of evacuees. He is not dressed for an office area, his ensemble a brown hooded sweatshirt and matching jogging pants. But that isn't what stands out most about this stranger.

It's that the man is *smiling*.

Smiling, watching as the people continue passing back and forth aimlessly: office workers, firefighters, emergency personnel. Each searching for where to go next. Watching as the chaos unfolds. Simply smiling. Delighted. He's *enjoying* this.

Jimmy can't believe it. What kind of sick bastard is he?

Jimmy and the man lock eyes on his way to the ferry. The man nodding as if a gentleman greeting a lady, tipping an imaginary cap. His smile growing wider still. Perplexing. Sickening. "What the??" There's no time to process the interaction. Jimmy must make that boat.

"Come on, all aboard!" calls the crewmate from the top of the boarding ramp, waving his arm to join the vessel. His pace quickens. "They won't leave me here. They *can't* leave me here." Jimmy sweating as he pounds the pavement in his brown leather shoes. His shins throbbing as they absorb the brunt of the impact.

Moments later, Jimmy thankfully hits the gangplank. "Glad you made it, we're almost at capacity. A few more minutes and you would have to wait for the next one." The crewmate briskly greets Jimmy as he steps aboard. His smile noticeably unlike that of man at the marina.

Jimmy weaves his way through the passengers, many of them trembling, as he seeks higher ground and fresh air on the upper level of the ferry.

Finally finding an open space, Jimmy sits down for the first time since he was at his desk compiling his daily task list. "Damn. That kid must have been close. Look at his face, like he saw a ghost or something." Two men standing above him comment on Jimmy's pale complexion and dilated pupils.

Shock fully setting in.

Jimmy hears them, but doesn't engage. Instead, working to gain his composure. As the shockwave sets in deeper, his hands shake uncontrollably. He looks down at his watch pulsating back and forth on his left wrist. Trying to focus on the time while his hands continue to quiver. Firmly grasping his wristwatch with his right hand finally steadies them both. At least long enough for him to check the time.

His watch reads 9:54 a.m. sixty-eight minutes. Everything changed in sixty-eight minutes. *Everything*.

9:59 a.m.

The South Tower of the World Trade Center collapses. Gasps and cries from nearly everyone aboard the ferry. His seat on the upper level provides him with a full view of the fall. Watching somberly as the spot he stood upon exiting the World Financial Center is now engulfed in an avalanche of steel, smoke and debris.

"Glad I moved. And thank God the ferry was still there." A fleeting moment of gratitude before his thinking shifts. "And I hope the bastard that was smiling about it isn't smiling anymore."

The ferry docks shortly thereafter in Hoboken. The feel is immediately different. For the first time all morning, Jimmy feels safe. The quiet of the quaint Hoboken streets doesn't compare to that of the emergency stairwell. It's time to walk home. To keep moving forward.

A few strangers stopping him along his route back to his brother Bryan's apartment. "Hey man, did you hear what happened?" they ask. "Yeah," he responds each time. "It's really bad." The people continuing on after that, nothing else to say. Seems like they just need to talk about what is happening. The inherent need to say something, anything, to help them understand. From their point of view, they couldn't possibly know his experience and the journey taken to reach these streets safely.

There are no wounds to treat. At least not ones anyone could see.

It's roughly a mile long walk across before he arrives back at his brother's condo building on First Street and Observer Highway. Wrestling with his keys before quietly opening the door to their shared one-bedroom apartment on the 9th floor.

The TV is on full volume, the newscast providing what information they have about the horrors in New York. He hears the shattered voice of one newswoman communicating details of another crash in Washington, D.C. and one more plane in Pennsylvania that went down in a field near a town called Shanksville.

Jimmy receiving a warm embrace from both Bryan and his girlfriend Casey, a flood of tears accompanying the bear hug. Casey nearly inconsolable as the tragedy continues to unfold.

"Glad you're home, bro," Bryan speaking first. "Thanks," Jimmy whispering in return, barely audible. The brothers together step out to the balcony of the apartment, a clear view of the smoke-filled lower Manhattan skyline from that vantage point. Only silence between them. Both fixating on the bizarre sight of a singular Tower gracing the skyline. Before today, this was Jimmy's favorite spot in the whole apartment, if not the world.

10:28 a.m.

Jimmy and Bryan watch from the balcony as the North Tower collapses. For them it is a soundless event, the image of the solitary tower from a moment ago gone now, joining its twin in a smoldering mountain of steel and glass. Only a few words shared between the brothers.

"Dear God. All those people…"

Shortly afterwards, Jimmy decides to lay down. Overwhelmed and exhausted, quickly falling asleep. As he closes his eyes, he lay hoping today is just one horrible nightmare. Maybe when he wakes up, today will start over. Maybe…

Unfortunately, for Jimmy and so many others, the nightmare of this beautiful Tuesday morning is real. And in a certain way, it's only beginning.

Return to Normalcy

3

The next morning, the brothers make the twenty-minute drive along the New Jersey Turnpike back to Bayonne. Staying at Mom's house for a few days before whatever might come next. Seems like the best option. Maybe distance will help.

Jimmy feels good being back in the old neighborhood. Friends and family are around. When he looks outside the front window of Mom's house, he doesn't see the burning remains of the Twin Towers. Instead, he sees green grass and childhood adventure.

Mom's house is situated on First Street, all the way at the southern tip of Bayonne. The beautiful green landscape outside the front window is Dennis P. Collins Park, where Jimmy spent nearly every day of every summer as a kid.

The special place in Jimmy's heart that holds the joyous memories and feelings of the World Trade Center has a twin as well, and Collins Park admirably holds the honor.

The park is nearly a mile long and nestled on the banks of the Kill van Kull, the waterway connecting Newark Bay with New York Bay and then the Atlantic Ocean beyond. Filled with pine trees, cherry blossoms, and basketball courts, along with a few playgrounds and oversized loveseat benches framing the most scenic viewpoints. But, best of all, the park's main attraction happens to be several of Jimmy's favorite grounds, baseball fields.

It's the kind of place where you can wander the various asphalt trails weaving through the green and always find something, whether it be new, unique or even something old that maybe you didn't notice the day before.

Now, Mom's house itself isn't much to brag about. Actually, it isn't even a house, it's a townhouse located on the western-most residential block of First Street. One in a row of five mid-century brick-faced homes squeezed together on the corner of the street. There isn't much space in each; a thousand square feet is generous, and even less space considering you can hear nearly everything happening in your neighbor's home, too. The thin plaster walls not offering much in the way of sound proofing.

Mom's townhouse is the second from the left when viewed from the street. Despite its limitations, it's a place Jimmy feels comfortable living in. It always has been because it's the only house Jimmy lived in from birth until college.

Aside from visions of playing professional baseball, Jimmy grew up dreaming of leaving here to experience life in New York City. But today, walking outside to the rolling green front lawn that is Collins Park feels a million miles away from Lower Manhattan. And for the first time he can remember, that's a good thing.

Quiet. Peaceful.

Just being in Bayonne is a relief. A gritty blue-collar town of sixty-thousand people. The city itself is a peninsula, bordering Jersey City to the north and surrounded by water thereafter, Newark Bay to the west, New York Bay to the east and the Kull to the south.

Generation after generation of families live here, Jimmy's being no different. Nearly all of Bayonne's residents are born here, work here or in neighboring Jersey City and eventually plan on dying there. The lucky few retire to the Jersey shore. The truly blessed are in Florida. Turns out, leaving is often the hardest part of living in Bayonne.

This town is quintessential Jersey. Italian delis, Irish pubs, middle class and public housing, Catholic, Jewish, Muslim. You name it, this place has it. Portraying the full spectrum of humanity across all races, creeds and colors. There's tremendous pride of place instilled in the residents of Bayonne. Or, according to a few of the more enlightened residents, the proper designation is the Golden Peninsula.

Blue-collar with a big heart.

Everyone knows everyone, or at least that's the way it seems. And for the larger immigrant family trees, it might appear that everyone is related in some way, shape or form. Folks from Bayonne are similar to other places in the world, too, preferring to keep their real life, their joys and fears, hidden behind the lace curtains adorning the windows.

Fight, scrap, grind, work— the common refrain of nearly every resident. That's what life here is about. Hard work and sacrifice are the two main ingredients to producing anything meaningful. "If it don't hurt, then it ain't worth it" would serve well as a mantra for the Golden Peninsula. Trust is by far the most precious commodity in town. Once gained, never wanting to lose it.

There is no celebration for the boys returning to town this week, no yellow ribbons on the street light in front on Mom's house for the prodigal sons that made the journey back to their birthplace. People too busy with an endless news cycle dominated by the September 11th attacks and the aftermath. The media these days a constant barrage of fear, sadness and despair.

During this time, as part of a collective national healing

process, the leaders of the nation call for a "return to normalcy". The refrain becomes ubiquitous on TV, newspaper and online. Yes, there's a growing call for "normalcy," served with a hefty dose of revenge.

"What does that mean for me? What's *normal* now?" Jimmy often thinking to himself on his solemn afternoon walks along the paths of Collins Park. Unable to speak to anyone about how he was feeling.

Too angry. Too sad. Too confused.

His thoughts now a long way away from attending the Florida/Tennessee football game. That feels like a lifetime ago. Thoughts still not far away from Quinn, however. When can I see her? *When?*

Friends and family continuously reaching out to help the healing process. Colleagues included. While in Bayonne, the human resources team from the firm puts him in touch with a trauma counselor. What a quick discussion that is.

Jimmy deciding to open up despite severe reservations. Informing the counselor of his experience from the day. The jumper. The smiling man. The ferry ride. The collapse of the Towers. "I'm sorry, sir. I don't know how to help you," the counselor soberly informs him. "Thanks for listening anyway. I appreciate you being straight with me." Click. End of session.

If he couldn't help, then who?

Connecting with Quinn nightly eases his fear and anxiety. Unfortunately, due to the travel restrictions following the attacks, they both know it will be a while before they would see each other. However, they remain true to a new evening ritual they fell upon. At the end of each long day and even longer night, Jimmy retreats to his childhood bedroom, sinking into the lumpy twin mattress that he grew too tall for years ago. Rolls over to face the wall that he shares with the neighbor next door as he dials Quinn from his cell phone, waiting to hear her tender voice on the other end. The faint green light from his cell phone now providing a guiding light in the darkness of his room.

Jimmy always dials the number from memory.

The ending of each night's conversation becomes part of the loving routine as well. The primary topic consistently returning to the stress of Jimmy's impending return to the city. Quinn's soft, loving voice, expressing her concern. "I'm worried you're taking this too fast. Really, are you sure you're feeling up to going back? Why not spend some more time at the house? They said you don't have to hurry back."

His response becoming automatic with each passing night: "I'm good. Seriously, I'm good. Not much for me in this town, anyways. Time to move on to the next thing. See what comes."

Never one to take the first answer that comes, Quinn tenderly presses her line of questioning, "Are you *sure*? Please promise me that you'll do something if you're not feeling good. I do wish you could talk to someone about this. I hope each night helps, but I think you might need more than just me."

"Yes, I promise. I'm okay. I've been thinking a lot about it, and I have an idea what this all means, of why it happened to me. And a big part of that is I'm lucky to be here, lucky that I have you. I get it. So yeah, I'm good. Ready to go back and keep things moving forward."

"Just know we need you to be more than okay. More than good. *We need you to be you.*"

"Thanks, beautiful. I'm working on it, promise."

"Okay, then. Get some rest. Goodnight. I love you."

"I love you too. Keep smiling." Click. Just as quickly as their loving interaction ends, Jimmy shifts to the dread of closing his eyes.

He's reluctant to share everything with Quinn.

The pervasive nightmare: the jumper speaking directly to him before his fall, Jimmy then paralyzed with fear in the exit stairwell of the World Fi building, causing him to miss the ferry. Watching from the edge of the marina as it safely crosses the Hudson River. Hearing rolling thunder behind him, turning to meet his end as the South Tower obliterates him while he stands motionless in front of the landslide.

The images haunting him during the day: men and women walking aimlessly in the park, covered in ash, bleeding, looking for a way home. Visions of mutilated corpses washing up on the shore of the Kill van Kull. Fragments of human remains. Any sound in the sky sending shutters through his spine. The immense feeling of sadness and loss. Slumping his shoulders under the weight of grief. A constant sense of being lost, a fog blanketing him.

Return to normalcy. Is *this* what normal is now?

No matter. Knowing he and Quinn are in love helps. Every bit of that thought counteracting his grief and pain. Quinn serving as an anchor, his connection to humanity. At this time, the only deep connection. How then, to move forward? What's the next step? The plan remains to return to work the Monday following the attacks. The commute to the city. The subway. Being in an office building again. Colleagues asking to talk. Or maybe even worse, no one wanting to talk to him.

Return to normalcy? Move forward.

The stories from the attacks and the tragedy of the lives impacted continuing to pour in during his days in Bayonne. Family and friends and the loved ones they lost. Quinn losing an uncle, a businessman working on the 99th floor of the South Tower. Also, a cousin, a firefighter from Brooklyn. One of the 343. Others they know losing family, friends and colleagues.

Jimmy becoming consumed by the stories of the first responders. Firefighters. Police. Port Authority. In awe of their bravery.

How will he show his?

Everyone feeling connected to the attacks and the tragedy in their own way. Through all the stories of loss his friends and family share, he is one of the few that people know was there. Jimmy struggling to know how to feel about that. How he *should* feel about that.

Without Quinn, his friends stepping up best to fill the void. Jimmy's "boys". The same group of kids that grew up together, navigated life together, played ball together and, through it all, stayed together.

An ever-resourceful crew, the boys manage to use the quiet time at home to visit their local watering hole. Every. Single. Night. Molly's is their version of *Cheers*. The place where everyone knows your name. With friends coming and going throughout the night like it's a house party, not a pub.

Jimmy's friend Jaws bartends there most nights. Aside from drinking more than he pours, Jaws is a perfect barkeep. A heart of gold that's quick with a joke and complete with an archive of utterly outlandish stories. Yup, that's right, good old Jaws hunts for greater kudu in the woods of Pennsylvania and recently saw a web-toed man kick an eighty-yard field goal. Just ask him, it's all "true".

As Jimmy opens the red wooden door to Molly's this particular night, Van Halen's "Running with the Devil" is playing on the jukebox. And that means one thing and one thing only: Jaws is running the shop tonight.

"Oh! Would you look at the tall drink of water that just walked in!" Jaws already a few rounds into his barkeep philosophy of "serve one, drink two" when Jimmy walks in. "You're on scholarship tonight my friend! A full ride, congratulations! What can I get you? Just make sure I like it too." Jaws releases a high-pitched cackle announcing the good news as Jimmy enters the front door.

"Thanks, Jaws. Not looking to get after it, though. Just want to be out."

"No problem. I'm working on a few tasty concoctions that you'll have to try later."

"Deal."

Each night, the topic of conversation at Molly's eventually turns to the attacks. And each time, the same comment is repeated to Jimmy once his story comes to light, often the result of one of the boy's sharing a little too much after drinking a little too much.

Unfortunately, tonight is no different than last night. Jimmy waits for the inevitable, "Damn man. You're lucky to be alive." His only answer a withdrawal to silence. Jimmy's closest friend, Casanova, quickly notices the somber mood shift and changes the topic to sports, beer, girls, whatever else. Anything else. Afterwards checking on Jimmy. "You okay man? I didn't think that would go there." Casanova offering solace.

"Yeah. All good Cas. It is what it is. They're right, though. I am just lucky to be alive."

"Cool." Just as quickly Casanova pivots his eyes. "Oh damn, you see those two girls just walk in? I'm going to pretend I'm an Australian stuck in the States without a place to stay. Maybe they'll take me home and provide me refuge?"

Jimmy laughs. "Yeah, good luck mate. I'll see you at the diner later."

The night with the boys ends the same way as all the others this week: a late-night feast at the 8th Street Diner. Sure enough, Casanova is the guest of honor this evening, comfortably finding refuge at the head of the table. Following the greasy spoon, his later-night phone call to Quinn. Their loving practice remaining steadfast throughout. Then, whatever sleep may come.

As night turns to day, part of the rhythm of Jimmy's life back in Bayonne becomes his afternoon walk in Collins Park. It feels good to move. Good to see green. And nice to be away from the TV or any conversations. The walks leave him alone to his thoughts. The wandering asphalt paths of the park giving structure and calmness to his otherwise scattered and restless musings.

Move forward. But how?

The training and conditioning of a Bayonne boy kicks in. Fight, scrap, grind and work through it. The attacks are now part of him. The story in his mind starting to write itself. You're a survivor. Don't talk about it. People don't want to hear it. Personify quiet fortitude instead. Move forward. An internal badge of honor. Just another obstacle life threw at you to overcome.

Remember this happened to you for a reason. This is just another part of what makes you who you are. Add it to the list: Dad, doubters that served as "coaches," Slav…whatever. Whoever. One question keeps creeping up though, nagging at him, really.

Is this really who I am? Store that away. You were meant to be there. To be part of the attack. To survive. This is who you are now. Be a survivor. Move forward. Quietly.

Jimmy continues his walks each afternoon. Enjoying the space. Enjoying diving deeper into creating his story of returning to normalcy. His plan expertly coming together. On Saturday afternoon, Jimmy again finds himself wandering towards his favorite path in the park, the one on the back side of the Pony League field leading towards the Little League complex. He loves these fields, the memories of the games and friendships they represent. His own field of dreams. Heck, a *whole park* of dreams. He finds himself smiling. First time in days.

Maybe it is a return to normalcy?

Always Here for You

———————

4

SUNDAY ARRIVES, TIME TO START PACKING UP AT
MOM'S HOUSE AND DRIVE BACK TO HOBOKEN.
TIME TO FACE THE VIEW FROM THE BALCONY.
TOMORROW MORNING'S COMMUTE INTO THE CITY:
PATH TRAIN, SUBWAY. THEN THE OFFICE AND HIS
TEAMMATES. PEOPLE CHECKING ON HIM TO FIND
OUT IF EVERYTHING IS OKAY. IF HE IS OKAY.

For Jimmy, it's time to prepare. Steel up. Know what you're
in for. This is who you are now. But first, one final walk in
the park. A farewell tour of sorts. Who knows where life will
take him now? What exactly the "new normal" will look like?
Moving forward doesn't mean coming back here, though. That,
he's sure of.

Tracking his chosen path in the park. Lost in his thoughts.
Picturing what tomorrow will bring and preparing his mind.
Preparing his story. Stick to the plan. Don't talk about it. People
don't want to hear about it. Stay strong. There's no *need* to
talk about it.

Be tough. Move forward. "Hey kid," a voice calls out from behind him.

Startling Jimmy, knocking him out of his vision for tomorrow morning and back to reality in Collins Park. The voice is familiar. The deep tone envelops the air with warmth. It's a comforting sound.

"Carpenter Joe?"

"Yup, it's me. And I almost forgot about that silly nickname."

Carpenter Joe.

**

Carpenter Joe is a member of what the boys referred to during their childhood as "the neighborhood nice guys". The neighborhood nice guys being a core group of four men that looked after the boys in a variety of ways.

They were older, either with grown kids of their own or without kids, but nevertheless always looking to help the straggly group of neighborhood youth. Genuinely caring about the boys. And the boys knew it. Like a personal neighborhood watch, each one committed to his part in helping the group of boys grow into men. Mutual respect flowing, but the boys still had to have some fun with it. And nicknames provide a unique ability to break down generational barriers. To the boys, these men are a dream team of adult sentinels. The roll call of distinguished members:

First up is Biscuits. Polish guy named, well, no one even attempted to pronounce his name because they couldn't find any vowels on his name tag, but he was always eating a biscuit for breakfast, so the name came naturally. He worked for the Parks Department. The oldest member of the group and forever dressed in his army green Parks Department uniform. Grizzled and missing his fair share of teeth, Biscuits was always quick with a smile and a corny joke.

His main responsibility was maintaining the grass in Collins Park. And he always made sure to mow the Pony League field first. That way the boys had a freshly manicured playing field for the whole day. A simple gesture, but one greatly appreciated; a fresh cut nearly always complete before the boys even finished breakfast. Biscuits loved tending to their field, then seeing the boys play for hours on end. No weeds to slow them down.

Next up, Salty. The hot dog man. Salty was the adjective best used to describe the brownish boiling water the dogs bathed in, not necessarily the man himself. Salty was skinny with a Marlboro Red permanently affixed to his lips and a matching Marlboro trucker hat adorning his head. Doesn't look like much and talks even less, but Salty was smart. Possessing an uncanny ability to read people in less than a second.

Salty fed the boys lunch every single day, all summer long, for years. Naturally introverted, so he never conversed with the boys much. But when someone was short money or the boys were vanquishing under a boiling hot summer sun, the kid still ate lunch and some extra waters were handed out, free of charge. He never asked for anything in return. Simply doing it because it was the right thing to do. Saying "thank you" always meant a lot to Salty, though. A wink and a slight bounce from the Marlboro said it all.

Then came Chopshop Charlie. A local barber who emigrated from Italy. The "chopshop" didn't come from being a barber per se, but rather from the frequency you left his shop not only with a fresh haircut, but with an actual fresh cut on your neck or ears.

No matter. Charlie loves the boys, always moving them ahead of any other customers at his shop. He wanted to see them outside playing, not inside with a bunch of old men talking sports or politics. Add in the fact some of the boys played "the beautiful game" of soccer only solidified their preferred status in the shop.

No one ever questioned Chopshop's policy for VIP customers. It was simply understood. Perhaps a slight fear of more than a nick keeping the other customers in check.

The final member of the neighborhood nice guys was Carpenter Joe. Not as old as the others, but old enough from the perspective of a group of kids. It's unclear if his real name is Joe or if one of the boys made that up, too, but "Carpenter Joe" sounded good, so they ran with it.

The kids heard he was a carpenter, so that part of the nickname came pretty easy. That, and his hands were *incredibly* strong and sandpaper rough. You would quickly learn that the hard way if you gave him a weak handshake. An unpolished granite vise grip making sure of that. The poor soul that gave Carpenter Joe a wet noodle greeting would have sore knuckles for days.

Carpenter Joe there for all bits of advice, both large and small. The small mostly revolving around baseball. Often noticing if a swing was off or a changeup grip could be adjusted. The large advice always something about life. Ever weaving the small and the large together seamlessly. Jimmy figured these are things carpenters are good at.

Mostly his lessons are about how failure and challenges are good things for them. Some of the boys listen, others could care less. The advice keeps coming, though. Carpenter Joe wants to help. Always.

***

Jimmy, turning and seeing his old friend from the neighborhood. Both grinning, happy to see each other. It had been a little while, but time wore on both of them well, despite the current circumstances.

"Come on, we gave up the nickname a long time ago, didn't we?"

"Yeah, I know. Figured I had to make sure it was really you."
Jimmy laughs and winks at the notion of a Carpenter Joe impostor.

Joe looks healthy, fit and trim. His hazel eyes and graying
hair evoking a distinguished manner. As per custom, Joe holds
a book in his hand. Cradling it in his left hand against his hip
as he walks. His book also standing the test of time quite well.

Jimmy never really thought Joe fit in around the neighborhood.
The other nice guys did, or they at least looked the part, but Joe
is a bit different. Come to think of it, though, he seems more a
part of the neighborhood than anyone.

Joe opens the conversation, "How are you, kid? I've heard
some things and hoped you might still be back in the neighborhood. I'm sorry to hear you were there."

"Thanks for that. I'm doing okay, I guess. Better."

"Mind if I join your walk? You know, like old times?"

This isn't the first time these two old friends took a walk on
these paths to discuss "things". The familiar feeling leaves
Jimmy a little lighter. "Sure. You're always welcome to join.
Since you're getting old, we'll walk slowly."

"Funny." Joe deadpanned. "But I'm not as old as I'm going
to be." Maybe a little diversion would help the story he wants
to tell Joe? Some humor? Jimmy files that idea away for later.

They walk; Joe listens. Jimmy seizing his first opportunity to
tell the story crafted in his mind. Immediately amazing himself
with how natural it sounds.

"They attacked us."

"I'm a survivor."

"No one can help or wants to listen. It's too sad, and they have
their own issues with it to worry about."

"I don't know why it happened to me, but it did. So, I'll deal
with it."

On and on. The story pouring out. Joe speaks only sparingly:

"I understand." "Okay." "I see." Eventually more details rushing out. Joe focusing intently on the words, and emotions, Jimmy shares. Telling Joe how he sees planes exploding in the sky that aren't there. Revealing to Joe about the jumper. Seeing him every night in his nightmare. Hearing the man speak to him before he jumps, "I have to do this. This is the only way home."

Revealing to Joe about the smiling man. How happy he was about the chaos, the madness, the death around them. How much the man enjoyed all of it. Evil personified. How the anger surges within him at the mere thought of the smiling man. Jimmy's eyes well up as he continues to speak. A stray tear falling down his rosy cheeks from time to time.

Joe continues to listen. Seeing the wounds come to the surface. Knowing full well the initial story is only going to bury them. Deep. "Thank you for sharing, kid. We've been through a lot over the years, you and me, and this is for sure the toughest test yet. I know this is hard. But I know you're strong."

"Thanks. I'll handle it."

"But will you *heal* it?"

The question stuns Jimmy. Heal? How the hell is *that* supposed to happen? "Huh? Say what?"

"You heard right. *Heal* it."

"Have you been listening? No one wants to *hear* about it, let alone heal it. Even the trauma counselor said he couldn't help, and now the carpenter knows better? I don't have time for this nonsense, Joe. It's not happening."

"Yes…I'm listening. I'll continue to listen. And I will always listen."

"Okay, then. Since you *are* listening. I'm moving forward. It happened. I'll deal with it. There's stuff I gotta do to get ready for the week. Time to move on. I'm going to take this and make something of myself." Jimmy visibly annoyed at the direction of the conversation.

"That's it, huh? Your story? Move on. Make something," Joe calmly replies.

"Yup. Haven't you heard? The world is moving on. They call it a return to normalcy. Everyone wanting everything to go back to the way it was. They sure don't want me stuck in the moment."

"This is going to take *time*, kid. And *courage*."

"Well, I don't have the time for it, Joe, I really don't. I gave it a few days back here in the park. That's enough. Now is the time for me to face what comes next; that's courage."

Joe obviously sensing the frustration in Jimmy's voice and in his eyes. Seeing the layers building in the tale he would tell. Perhaps now isn't the time. But if not now, *when*? Sad that the conversation turned this way, Joe feels it best not to push further. Perhaps there will come another time to press on. "Kid, let me tell you one more thing before you move forward."

"Of course. Go ahead." Frustrated, but realizing Joe is trying to help. As always. "What is it?"

"Not what. Who." Joe continuing. "You'll never be the person you are meant to be, *the very best of who you truly are,* until you choose to heal this. Never. I know none of this makes sense for a lot of people, not just you. But there's always a reason behind what happens in life and how it happens *for* you. I believe you know that. And I hope you find it once again. I hope that you remember the source of courage."

Jimmy flips. "*For?* Seriously? *For?!* No thanks, Joe. I'm not buying it. This isn't like the things we talked about when I was kid. This is real-world grown-up stuff, so it's time to look at it like a real-world grown-up does. That was a direct hit *to* us, *to* those people that were killed, *to* me. Those bastards wanted me dead. Guess what? Screw 'em. I'm here. And they can't defeat me. I know exactly who I am and where I'm going. Happens *for*? Come on. That's garbage."

Joe pauses before engaging the charged response Jimmy unleashed. "I hope so, kid. I sure hope you know. Because you're the only one with the answer to who you are. The only one with the ability to find the truth. If you seek, you will find what lies at the core."

Knowing the conversation went sour, Jimmy doesn't want to leave it this way. Joe simply trying to help, same as always, but this time it's hard to swallow. Painful even. Nevertheless, he doesn't want to burn the bridge between them. Jimmy takes a breath, extending the exhale. "I'll think about it, Joe. I do appreciate you taking the walk and listening, as always."

"I as well, kid. Take care of yourself now. I'll be here if you ever need anything, as always. Now you better be getting out of here. It sounds like you have a lot to do in order to get ready for tomorrow. I wish you well with all those big plans ahead."

It pains Joe to say those words. They just feel wrong. He wants to help, but didn't. Couldn't. Did he miss his chance?

"Thanks Joe. I'll see you around," a contrite Jimmy replies. The two friends shake hands at a fork in the path. Each choosing their separate way home from that point. Joe sits on the bench behind the fir tree opening his book, Jimmy taking a path to the right. Back to Mom's house to finish packing up.

It would be eighteen years before the close friends would see each other again.

SECTION TWO

One Step Back, Two Steps Forward?

The Prodigal Son

5

MID-AUTUMN IN 2019. THE SUN IS SHINING, BLUE
SKIES ABOVE WITH ONLY A SCATTERING OF FEATHERY
CLOUDS MIXED IN. THE AIR IS CRISP AND COOL WITH
A MILD BREEZE, ENOUGH FOR A LIGHT JACKET. THE
FRIGID WINTER AIR OF THE NORTHEAST STILL FAR
OFF IN THE DISTANCE.

For all intents and purposes, a beautiful Fall day. Much like
it was all those years ago.

Jimmy is back in Bayonne, at a church of all places. St.
Andrew's Roman Catholic Church to be exact. Located on 4th
Street and Broadway, the outer edge of the old neighborhood.

Being in Bayonne is not something that happened frequently
in the intervening years. Mostly by choice, but mainly because
life picked up speed in the years following September 11th. Like
many people, a dizzying blur of questions and answers. The
who, what and where of growing into adulthood— who to marry,
what to do for a career and where to live— as we shape our lives.

Marriage to Quinn in 2007. The realized dream of a successful
long-distance relationship. Through the years following that

same feeling remaining, each day feeling like the beginning of another great adventure. The legend and beauty of Quinn's smile growing in grace and splendor with each passing year. Jimmy as enamored with her today as he was when they first met.

In the decade following their wedding, both their family and Jimmy's career grew. Welcoming four children of their own, two boys and two girls, and all that comes with becoming a parent. Including lots of love and lots less sleep.

Jimmy himself climbing the corporate ladder from a senior accountant to a Managing Director at a prestigious international investment firm. "Due diligence" and "hedge funds". That's all really anyone back home ever knew about what he did for a living. Sounds fancy enough. And he looked the part as well, donning pinstripe suits, cufflinks and power ties. And he worked enough too, long hours and near constant global travel. Stress and a mobile device becoming ever-present companions, even in the delivery room at the birth of his children.

During that time, Quinn blossoming into a mother far greater than Jimmy a Managing Director. The family pillar, a bedrock foundation of strength and grace. If it weren't for her, who knows how different things might be for all of them. Stepping away from her career in Oncology in order to move towards creating the life Jimmy and Quinn so often spoke of creating together.

Yes, Jimmy went back to New York City the Monday after the attacks. Told that story of surviving, of being at "Ground Zero" as it came to be known, to himself over and over again. Taking that story and indeed making something of himself. Ever-weaving the internal narrative of how he could overcome what happened to him.

The year following September 11th, his accounting firm failing, the result of a criminal indictment of obstruction of justice against the company itself. It turns out that "creative" and "accounting" aren't necessarily two words that go together. As a result, Jimmy finding himself inside one of the largest corporate failures in modern history.

"Not the worst day I've ever had in the office," telling himself as panic and fear of the unknown engulf the firm. The unrelenting tide of events sweeping away careers, reputations and financial wellbeing for so many.

Keep moving forward. Take the scattered pieces of what happens to you and make something of yourself. Jimmy parlaying that experience into a career that took off just as fast as the new firm he joined. A match seemingly born of destiny.

In retrospect, the years between his last meaningful visit to Bayonne and now were good. Ups, downs, twists and turns— sure. But all in all, life is good. Nevertheless, on this brisk Fall day he is back in Bayonne, on a weekday no less. No longer working for his major firm, traveling around the world or even commuting to the City.

Change transpiring for Jimmy and the family. It was time.

Now finding himself back in town for the reason most people come back to Bayonne: a funeral. A family friend passing of cancer, Jimmy and Quinn wanting to be there for support. An obligation of sorts.

St. Andrew's is a magnificent church. Antique stained-glass windows, rustic oak pews and three-dimensional carvings of the Stations of the Cross lining the walls. It is, by all accounts, a fitting place to honor someone.

Jimmy wistfully recalling the Sunday night masses there with the boys, nostalgia washing over him as he fiddles with the hymnal during the ceremony. They didn't behave like choir boys, far from it at times, actually, but at least they were there. And being there has to count for something in God's eyes, doesn't it?

The departed is a former member of the military, having served in the Navy before a notable career as a local fireman. At the conclusion of the ceremony, the patrons file out of the church and stand shoulder to shoulder as the color guard plays taps to honor the fallen and his service to our country. Jimmy barely knows the deceased, yet still grows emotional at the offering of the dutifully folded American flag to the family. The family embracing the young soldier following his presentation of gratitude and respect.

Following the color guard, an announcement from the funeral director, "The family asks attendees to gather at The Burning Man Tavern on First Street. They deem it a customary conclusion for this loving and large Irish-American family. Please join them in celebration."

Jimmy smiles coyly. No funeral or wedding or birthday party (and, as he can attest, even a child's first birthday party) would be complete for this family without a fair share of Ireland's famous imports.

Also laughing at the notion of visiting The Burning Man. Primarily because of where it's located, on the western most edge of First Street, under the bridge at the end of a desolate stretch of blacktop. It's the last block on First Street and follows past the one he grew up on. The Burning Man is the only occupied building on that entire stretch of town now. Everything else around it gone for years after the oil refinery across the street shut down.

But the name, though, The Burning Man, that's as Bayonne as it gets. The place used to be called The Steel Arches, an homage to the bridge hovering overhead. Arches was a working man's pub if there ever was one, the oak floors layered in soot and ash from the day's labor across the street. The place sold only beer and whiskey. No brands, just bottles labeled "beer" and "whiskey". The fridge was for beer; the glasses were for whiskey.

Heaven help the man that asked for something different. Rarely would a woman ever set foot in there, except to find her husband and drag him home after being out too long. Kids weren't even allowed to peek in the windows.

There's no spiritual or historical significance to the new name, though. Rather, it's a mix of gallows humor and local legend. You see, for decades, the refinery across the street operated as functioning toxic wasteland. Ultimately closed and dismantled during Jimmy's childhood by the government, who left the site abandoned to continually poison the soil and water. A rusted chain link fence was all that was left behind to secure the perimeter. The bar on the opposite corner was the only building left standing once demolition was complete.

Local legend tells that several years ago, one Steel Arches happy hour patron had a few too many and wandered from the bar in the early evening, presumably to walk it off before returning home. However, his friends spotted something rather peculiar upon leaving the pub several hours later. An emerald green silhouette wondering the grounds of the old refinery. Upon further inspection, the apparition was their friend, a radioactive glow emanating from him as he walked aimlessly in the contaminated pasture.

The Steel Arches giving birth to The Burning Man.

"Okay, we'll see you over there," Quinn says to her mother and sister, confirming their attendance at the repass.

"I'll drive." Jimmy smiles as he dangles the keys to their time-tested Black Jeep Grand Cherokee for the trip to the outer reaches of downtown. "Be my guest. You know the way better than most." Quinn extends her hand and returns Jimmy's smile with a loving one of her own.

The ride to the pub serves as scenic tour of Jimmy's old stomping grounds. A block away from St. Andrew's is Chopshop

Charlie's old place. Different owner now, Charlie retiring to Florida years ago. Just as the boys graduated college. They probably don't do VIP customers anymore. That's a shame, but hopefully they no longer hand out band-aids after haircuts either.

Jimmy rubs his neck as he and Quinn drive passed the storefront. The lingering effect of a few too many close shaves. "Thanks, Chops." Offering a brief glance in the rearview mirror to assess if he is due for another haircut soon.

A few blocks south, the jeep turns right at Broadway and First Street, Collins Park now coming into full view. The sun high overhead illuminating the green fields, winding black asphalt paths and the water's edge beyond. The trip across town allows for an end-to-end expedition of the park.

On the drive across First Street to the pub, Jimmy's eyes, and mind, wander from the road over to the park. Considering it wasn't even noon, and not exactly feeling up for a few hours' worth of drinks on a weekday, he instead offers an alternative plan.

"Mind if I take a walk in the park instead of heading to the bar?" he asks Quinn. "It's been a while."

"No, not at all. I'm not feeling well, so I'm not looking to make this a long stay. I'll go say hello to everyone. Plus, it will give me a good reason to skip the drinks in order to pick you up," Quinn answers with a wink and her legendary smile. Finishing her comment off, "Enjoy the time."

"Thanks. Appreciate that."

Now cruising by Salty's old spot. Right behind home plate of the softball field. No one ever took the spot after Salty passed. In Jimmy's mind, no one ever could. A momentary rumble in his stomach follows. It is closing in on lunch time, and a Salty Dog would do wonders right now. Laughing to himself, even his stomach knows exactly where he is. Some habits really do die hard.

The black Grand Cherokee continuing down First Street towards the pub. Pulling over for a scheduled stop at the Pony League field near Mom's house. "Text me when you want me to pick you up. I'll meet you here." Quinn drops him off with a delicate kiss. "Oh, and one more thing. Behave yourself, too. We all know what you're capable of in this park!"

A burst of laughter. "I got it. Best behavior. I promise. Love you. Keep Smilin'."

Quinn pulls away from the curb, joining the motorcade of cars on their way to The Burning Man. Jimmy stops for a moment to survey the landscape before crossing the street and entering the park.

Inhaling a deep breath in, bringing in the air, the smells, the sunshine. Processing all of the surroundings in order to gather his bearings after the years away. He's dressed formally for a casual stroll: pressed tan pants, a white button-down shirt under a maroon sweater. Navy blue jacket and tan leather boots rounding out his ensemble.

Feeling as if he stepped back in time. Everything familiar. Everything feeling like home.

Some changes to the grounds, but merely cosmetic. A few of the trees are different, old plantings giving way to new growth. Thankfully, the parks department removing the thorny shrubs nearest to the Pony League entrance. Replacing them with a row of colorful flowers. Those shrubs would take their fair share of skin when you walk by them, and even more when you fetch a foul ball stuck inside.

The old shrubs bringing Biscuits to mind. "Wonder what he would think of the flowers? Probably would make some corny joke about a bouquet. The field looks like it could use a bit of trim, though. Guess they don't make 'em like Biscuits anymore." Like his fellow guardian Salty, Biscuits is long gone now, passing years ago when the boys were in high school. They all attended his funeral, too. The only members of the congregation under the age of sixty.

Walking through the park, noticing new benches added to enhance the scenic viewpoint of the Bayonne Bridge. They look ideal for wedding pictures or holiday cards. Some of the outside changed, sure. But the soul of the place is still the same. It is welcoming and warm, despite the coolness of a mid-Autumn day. Jimmy can feel it. Half a lifetime spent playing, laughing, fighting, crying, climbing trees and fences, exploring every square inch of this playland. The memories all washing over him in a profound wave of peace. Smiling effortlessly.

The park does feel a bit smaller than when he was younger. Presumably, that's what happens with age and a fair bit of travel. After all, this isn't exactly London's Hyde Park. What was once a wide-open land full of promise feels quaint now. No matter the size, though, it still feels like home. Like *home*.

An instinctive calling to the winding path that rounds passed the Pony League field, a baseball field that was as close to a second home growing up as there ever could be. "Ah, my old path," Jimmy thinks to himself, smile widening. He knows it well. Easy to visualize where it leads. The black asphalt would wind behind home plate and turn right towards the Bayonne Bridge, bearing slightly left, then right again behind the Little League field. Splitting and reconnecting at several points along the way.

Traveled it thousands of times as kid. Now a Memory Lane come to life.

Almost immediately upon taking the first step, his thoughts spin into high gear. Jimmy's mind bouncing around like a caffeinated monkey. Quinn. The kids. What to do next? He made a huge life decision recently. One that felt right in every way. Only one thing was really missing. Something BIG.

Do I really *know* what I'm doing?

Sure, there are plans. Some more concrete than others. Still, that thought gnaws at him today. And many days before this one too. "Do I have what it takes? Can I even do this?" Maybe it was the funeral. Those always mess with people, don't they?

More questions enter the chorus. "Am I living fully? How do I even know that answer? Absolutely, look at the change I made, *we* made. Beyond bold."

That answer rings hollow.

The questions continue to nag him as he walks his familiar path. Silently eating away at him at home, only growing louder now in the silence of the park. He knows it, too. No longer connecting with Quinn the same way as when they're at their best. Being short with the kids. Agitated. Stressed. Unsure.

Ugh. "What the *hell* is going on? I made the right decision. I know it. So why am I stuck? Why can't I move forward?" Continuing on the path. Head down, walking on auto-pilot. Trying to focus, to breathe deeper, calm his mind. Find the answer.

He spent the last few years learning techniques to find clarity. To cut through the noise and nonsense. That's how he found his answer of what to do in life. To leave his career. Pursue his passions. Pursue more time with family. "UGH! *Dammit.* Where do I go from here? Why isn't this working?" The internal noise deafening.

"You still haven't answered the real question yet, have you?" shoots a voice from beside him.

Jimmy stops cold. Instantly recognizing the voice.

"Holy sh…. *Joe*? That you?"

"Yeah, kid. Still here." A gentle smile rolls across Joe's grizzled stubble, his hazel eyes still full of life. Even now his athletic physique apparent underneath a white Henley shirt, houndstooth coat and navy-blue trousers. His hair is more salt than pepper compared to all those years ago, but still visible under his news-boy cap. Left hand ever clutching that book, resting gently near his hip. The book a bit more weathered than the last time the two friends were together. Joe appears decidely less weathered than his accompaniment.

Good to see one of the neighborhood nice guys is still on guard.

Joe carries that same mystique. The aura Jimmy nor any of the other kids in the neighborhood could ever explain. He just makes you *feel* better.

"Been a while. How have you been, kid? And what might it be that brings you back around these parts?"

Stunned. It takes a few seconds for Jimmy to find the words. "A…a…a…funeral. Family friend. Just figured I'd get some air and take a walk around here." Pausing. Jimmy gathers himself and the moment he finds himself in. "You're right, though. It's been a while." Feelings of regret and guilt underlying his words. Jimmy pauses yet again. "Damn Joe. It's good to see you."

"You as well. I'm sorry for your loss."

"Thanks for that. I'm sure the family would appreciate it." Glancing upwards and meeting Joe's eyes. "Care to take a walk with me?" Jimmy asks sheepishly.

"Of course, kid. Let's walk. Just like old times." Side by side again. Jimmy taking his customary spot to the right, same as always.

"Just like old times. Just not like last time." Remorse from their blow-up all those years ago still fresh in Jimmy's mind. Joe waves his hand, as if swatting a fly, not saying a word. With that simple gesture, the pain of their last encounter drifts away.

The late morning sun shines brightly on the two old friends. A cool breeze blowing off the water. A beautiful day for a walk in the park. Finding themselves back on the winding path trailing behind the Little League field. Following the course around the bend, Jimmy fills Joe in on all of life's happenings since they last met. It is an abbreviated version, but still packed with details of Jimmy's life. Of what happened after he chose to move forward.

"Quinn and I..."

"You're still together! Oh, that's wonderful to hear kid. You two always seemed meant for each other." Jimmy realizes quickly how long it's been. How much of life really happened since they last spoke.

First, he found love. Profoundly deep love with Quinn. Soulmate level. "Yes, we are. Married back in '07. All of the boys served as groomsmen at our wedding. That was one amazing night. We even managed to find a bagpipe band to ignite the festivities. And it's been incredible ever since."

Children, including their troubles in conception. "It was back in September '08. The markets were crashing, and I had no idea about my job or whether the firm would make it. Then, on top of that, a doctor tells us that I will never be able to have children." Jimmy pauses, reflecting on memories he hasn't visited in quite some time. "Sheesh, that was a difficult time. We made it through, though. Well, in reality, Quinn pulled us through."

Joe senses the significance of that moment in time, wishing he knew the answer before he asks, "Do you have children now?"

Jimmy reflexively smiles as he pictures his children in his mind. "Yeah, we've been blessed with four of them. Boy, girl, boy, girl, in that order. I guess a small part of me still doesn't mind proving other people wrong, huh Joe?" Both men laugh at the comment before Jimmy describes life at home. "Wild. Chaotic. Joyous. We're a family alright." The pride of fatherhood pours out while recalling their ages: 10, 8, 4, and 2. Then their various interests: ice hockey, soccer, Legos, superheroes and princesses.

"We're in the middle of it…right in the soup." Jimmy says with another heartful laugh and an even bigger smile.

Turning to his career next. The fall of his accounting firm after he returned to New York. And how a fortuitous elevator ride following the collapse landed him at a relatively young firm. Small in size, but big in potential.

How that matured into a job and a firm he loved. Traveling the world, creating teams and building a business. Relishing each aspect of the opportunity. More than anything, though, it was the amazing relationships. He has friends, not colleagues. The kind you have for life.

His tenure saw the business experience exponential growth, followed by the Financial Crisis, then growth again, but with all the after effects. A supportive environment morphing into a shark tank. In order for him to advance further up the ladder, he was ordered to "punish people" and "take others out." What began as a job and evolved into a career turned into work. Then something unrecognizable.

Jimmy unveiling the cycles of life and career in all their beauty, both good and bad.

"That's one heck of a ride, kid. I'm happy for you, for the life you've built. Now I see why it's taken you a while to come back."

"I tried…"

"No need, kid. We're here now." Joe's right hand shoots up, stopping Jimmy's sentence in its tracks. "I imagine to the outside world it seems like you have it all figured out. So, what brings you back to this old place?"

Jimmy lets out a faint sigh before answering, "I'm not exactly sure what to do next."

"Well, how about we keep walking down this path together until Quinn picks you up."

"Ha. Yeah, guess that seems like a good place to start."

"Just stating the obvious. Who knows, maybe we'll come up with something along the way."

"Joe, I honestly just feel *stuck*. Do you have any tools to help?"

"Tools?" Joe looks baffled at the idea.

"Yeah, tools. A while ago, I started doing things like breathing exercises, gratitude journaling, eating better. You have anything like that? Something to help me fix this?"

"Fixing implies something is broken. And I don't see anything like that in front of me."

"Come on, Joe. After all the advice through the years. You have to have something for life now, don't you?"

"Sure." Jimmy is immediately relieved to hear his mentor might have a solution. "I have three things. First, I have a book." Joe lifts his left hand to present his most famous accessory.

"What's in here." Pointing to his heart. "And one more thing that might help."

"What's that?" Jimmy flattened by the first two responses, expecting much more from Joe. Now eagerly trying to solve the trifecta puzzle.

"A chisel."

"Huh? A chisel?"

"Yes, a chisel." Jimmy chuckles at the image of his mentor carrying around a rusty old chisel. Although given his trade, it does at least seem mildly plausible.

"Is that funny?"

"Sort of. What else are you carrying around in those pockets? Let's just say I don't know how a chisel goes with the first two. And I don't know how it helps me with my next move."

"Chisels are able to turn the hardest substances on earth into beautiful works of art. Maybe even more than beautiful, depending on how you look at them."

Jimmy in expressionless. "Wonderful. How about we focus on the first two though. They feel more appropriate."

"As you wish. But is that truly how you're thinking about this? Your next move? This isn't checkers, chess or even baseball, kid. It's *life*." Joe continues. "So, let me ask you something then, if you don't mind. What were you looking for all this time?"

Jimmy is confused by the question. And perhaps even more so by the answer. "I wanted to create something far different than what I grew up with. I wanted to make something of myself. To be a success story from this place."

"It appears you were successful at creating something indeed. And yet you are right back here, on this simple little patch of asphalt. Curious." Joe stays on the topic, "So you mentioned that you wanted to *be* a 'success', tell me please, what's that mean to you?"

Jimmy gives Joe a mildly dumbfounded look. "Seriously, Joe? All the things I mentioned before: marriage, family, house, job, money. To have what everyone else has. That's what success looks like."

"Sounds like a common definition." Joe takes a moment. Allowing time and space for the words to seep below the surface of the conversation: "So, then, what brought about all of this change? The change that has you stuck, broken and common."

Jimmy flinching backwards, feebly attempting to avoid the verbal counter punch. "Ouch. Damn, man. You didn't have to go there."

"You asked me if I had tools to help fix something that isn't broken in order to get you unstuck from a successful life that you created in order to be like everyone else."

Jimmy takes in a deep breath and exhales. "I guess I did, didn't I?"

"Let's honor the truth instead of condemning the seeker, shall we? Perhaps then now is a good time to discuss what spurred the change."

"Yeah, now does seem like a good time." Jimmy quietly answers Joe, while still mentally reflecting on what he's asked of his mentor. "Well, I haven't told anyone this part of it before. But one night, I snuck home early during the week so I could see everyone awake, I was hoping for a real family dinner kind of night. As soon as I got home, I cooked up some burgers on the grill. Still had my suit on too. And as we sat together, I looked around our dinner table and noticed I was surrounded by everyone laughing and enjoying simply being with one another. Then I realized something."

"And that is?"

"I was the only person sitting there that had no idea who they were. And each day, I went to grind away in the office for countless hours so someone else could pass judgement on my ideas, measure my contributions as worthy. And each day, I was moving further away from the same knowing they had. As I sat there, a big part of me grew dim. Then, when I looked up again at every else, I realized the only thing I really knew was that I was *the lie* at the table." Jimmy takes a short breath before expanding on the story. "And as I kept sitting there with everyone smiling, everything else around me went quiet. I could see, but couldn't hear. Then a thought came: one day, these kids are going to call me out on it. They are going to grow up and call BS on me telling them they could be anything they wanted in this world. And they would be right, and I would have no response. I *hated* that feeling. I felt like a fraud. A ghost in a suit."

"That's a powerful moment of awareness. I acknowledge that. So, I take it that's what sparked the change?"

"No. Something worse came to mind after that." Joe is

intrigued, raising his eyebrows towards his salt and pepper hairline, the wrinkles in his forehead disappearing under the brim of his cap. "And what might that be?"

"What if they *didn't?* What if they grew up and never said a word to me about it? And I sat there as the years went by watching as their light grew dimmer, hopes and dreams giving way to 'reality' and what they were 'supposed' to do. Too afraid to say anything to them about it. Too afraid because *I* was their role model. They would live what they thought was a good life, only it wasn't *their best life*. It was like I saw the future happening as they sat there as children. I knew right then and there that's not who I wanted to be. Not the father or husband I was going to be."

"And that is who you are now?"

Jimmy's head tilts. "I thought I knew. Turns out I'm not so sure about that." Feeling exposed, but not ashamed, of his answer.

"Well, perhaps we start with who you want that person to look like?"

"I really don't know, to be honest. I just know who I don't want him to look like: that ghost in a suit. The person that drifts around and never feels like they're in the right place no matter where they are."

"Let's keep going then. There's a big difference between the worlds of knowing what you don't want versus knowing what you do want. The universe provides what you focus on, it doesn't differentiate between do and don't."

"But what if that person isn't great in the eyes of Quinn and the kids? What if they want the 'old me' back?"

"Do you really believe that?"

"No. I don't." Jimmy embarrassingly glances towards the ground. Finally saying aloud what he already knows inside.

Silence follows. Their walk continues that way for several minutes. Neither man speaking. The birds above and the rustle of the nearby dog park providing the background to the pause in conversation. Finally, Joe breaks the quiet. Calmly, yet forcefully. "You were once resolute that other people wouldn't define your life, put you in a box with boundaries and limits. You were determined not to fall prey to common sayings masking themselves as truths."

Pursing his lips and narrowing his eyes, Jimmy calculates his response, unsure exactly what to say next. "All those other things were a long time ago. I thought I was meant to live a good life. To provide a good life for my family."

"Destiny doesn't arrive from living a good life. It arrives as you live the life you were *meant for*."

Jimmy soaks in the words from his mentor. After all these years, he still feels like a wide-eyed kid hearing something new for the very first time.

Joe moves forward, both physically on the path and in the conversation. "This has nothing to do with your family, nothing; it has everything to do with you. Who *you* are. The real question. The one that evidently still requires an answer." Deflated. Jimmy gazes up at Joe after kicking a few rocks gathered on the path, "I know."

"Come, let's keep walking. Perhaps we'll come across an apple tree." A sly wink accompanying Joe's invitation.

The Apple Tree

6

JULY IN THE SUMMER OF '88 IS HOT. 100 DEGREES IN
THE SHADE KIND OF HOT. A SUFFOCATING BLANKET
OF URBAN HUMIDITY. THE THICK, STEW-LIKE AIR
LEAVING ITS MARK ON FOREHEADS AND CLOTHES
CONSTANTLY SOAKED WITH SWEAT.

Thank goodness for the water fountains in the park and the
shade of the trees. If it wasn't for those simple amenities, the
boys would wilt away under the scorching summer sun. But
despite the heat, the thirst and the sunburn, summer remains the
best time of year. Jimmy walks lighter than the air; a permanent
smile stretches ear to ear. It's easy to laugh and enjoy these days.

Freedom. Boundless and untamed freedom of youth. Very
few possessions are required for this level of enjoyment. A
baseball glove; Jimmy's tan beaten up Rawlings with a Dale
Murphy autograph etched in the pocket. A bat; Bryan's hand-
me-down Easton Black Magic measuring twenty-nine inches. A
tennis ball and a bike. A black Mongoose with pegs on the front
and back. Another generous Bryan hand-me-down. Maybe a
few dollars stuffed into his sock for safekeeping, or for a hot
dog and a water.

Summer. In Bayonne. Heaven on Earth.

Nowhere is the melting pot of Bayonne on full display more than during the summer. And nothing is more emblematic of that diversity than the soundtrack of life during these hazy and humid days: from Bon Jovi and Bruce Springsteen to Public Enemy and Rob Base. Classic Rock, Rap, Hair Bands, whatever. Jimmy's personal favorite this summer? "Bring the Noise" by Public Enemy.

Everyone keeps playing the music. And playing it loud.

Even the grittiness of Bayonne lightens up when school is out. Nothing but sunshine, warm weather and ball to play. All day, every day. Baseball is mainly the game of choice. Each day the boys playing out their major league fantasy on a Field of Dreams perfectly manicured by Biscuits, the older guy from the Parks Department that cuts the grass.

The boys befriended him earlier this summer. They patiently were waiting on the bleachers for him to complete the morning cut. As he drove through the oversized gate on the giant green tractor, the boys applauded a job expertly well done. They were grateful for the shorter grass, and at the same time, amazed the man was operating a multi-ton piece of machinery with just his right hand. His left hand was reserved for a more important mobile amenity, a fresh biscuit.

"That dude is eating a friggin' biscuit driving a tractor like it's a Power Wheels!" Jimmy's friend Money Man pointed out for all the boys to hear. "You guys see this?!"

"Thanks for the cut Biscuits!" The Colonel shouted as the man drove by to rousing applause.

"You're welcome boys. Hey, which one of you is a pitcher?" A half-tooth smile accompanying the question from Biscuits, who didn't seem to mind the nickname at all.

"Me?" Jimmy responded not entirely understanding the question.

"Then you should be carrying all the water!" Biscuits laughed himself nearly straight off his seat as his joke failed to find a home with the boys. Regardless, Biscuits enjoyed having an audience for his brief comedy routine. So much so, he continued hooting as he rumbled on to the next patch of grass to manicure.

From that point forward, the Pony League field would receive the first cut of the day.

Sure, Jimmy and the boys mix in other sports sometimes too, such as basketball, whiffle ball, soccer and tennis. Occasionally, even a pool-break during the afternoon just to avoid full melt-down. Whatever keeps a small group of ten-year-old boys moving and outside is best. Combine a ball and some healthy, and at times unhealthy, competition, and it's a recipe for their very own wonder years.

All of the boys have nicknames, some earned, some given: Sweetness, Casanova, the Colonel, Money Man, Soup, Big Smooth, Kermit, Spoon (Soup's younger brother), Broomstick and Jaws. Real names saved for parental discipline. Each moniker evolving out of a unique set of circumstances. So much so they would require a set of stories in and of themselves.

Oddly enough, the only one without a nickname is Jimmy.

They are from all different backgrounds; racial, economic, social. A living testament to the diversity of their birth city. Many of the boys are known as "2nd Gens", meaning they're second generation Americans. Their grandparents immigrating to the U.S. in the early part of the 20th century. Some during the time of the Great Depression and others earlier than that. They hail from all across Europe: Ireland, Italy, Germany, Poland, France, Spain.

Others in the crew are also immigrants, but of a more recent timeline. Their lineage is primarily Hispanic: Dominican, Puerto Rican, Cuban. Naturally, just to mess with everyone else from time to time, they speak only Spanish to each other. Although, this does come in handy for all the boys, as it vastly expands their cursing vocabulary.

The Black kids in the crew would often point out that none of them, *none*, ever visited the countries they were so proud of. So, whenever an argument of Irish versus Italian or some variation would emerge, a voice of reason would chime in to quell the matter.

Soup in particular always enjoys identifying nonsense and calling it as he sees it.

"Y'all are ridiculous, you know that? My dad eats pasta and drinks beer too. But he sure as shit ain't Italian or Irish. And he doesn't want to be, either. He just likes pasta and beer."

Or more pointedly...

"You don't do stupid stuff because your grandma's Polish, so don't go blaming her for that. And I know her; she's a great woman! And you know what else? She's really smart, too. You're just a dumbass."

Spoon normally wouldn't let any of his older brother's wisdom pass without a "sho nuff" for emphasis. The timing of his exclamation points nearly bordering on supernatural.

No one in the rest of the crew had any disagreement with Soup's logic or rationale. Usually, that level of understanding and insight just ends the argument. Albeit temporarily.

Regardless of the plain truth that they were all born in this same town, in New Jersey no less, each of the boys are extremely proud of their heritage and the unique traits it provides them with to experience the world. Their differences don't divide them, in fact, they are what make the group whole. Bright futures await the full lot of them: doctors, teachers, mechanics, lawyers, businessmen…even a D.E.A. agent and an underwater welding expert.

The future can wait though. Summer time as a kid is for playing ball and having fun.

Picking Jimmy out of line-up in 1988 isn't terribly difficult; brown hair with a tinge of ginger, weighing roughly sixty pounds soaking wet, and blessed with a complexion that is both ghostly pale and freckle-faced. He's a human string bean with a thick Jersey accent. Complementing the look are a Coke-bottle thick set of glasses and a farmer's tan that's a walking endorsement for Coppertone sunblock. Jimmy always completes each summer's ensemble with a hat from a Major League Baseball team; this summer's choice? The Montreal Expos. No particular reason why…red, white and blue colors, perhaps.

None of the boys' backgrounds or looks matter, though. Merely small details for them in the grand scheme of life. Friendship is what matters on these fields and in these streets. Being boys is what matters.

Rarely discussing anything outside of ball, well, except of course to find someone to make fun of for the day. Everyone takes their turn. "Takes" being the operative word there. The only thing providing more heat than the blazing sun above is the burning spotlight of ridicule that will find you sooner or later.

Two rules apply to any and all insults. One: No comments about moms or sisters. Two: Don't take it personal. You want to survive in this town? You need thick skin. And you need to know how to take a joke.

Day after day, the group of boys roll along to the rhythm of summer. Sunrise to sunset. Each day when the sun shines, Collins Park is the place to be. But as the sun sets and the evening takes center stage, the spot to be shifts to the Little League stadium.

The Bayonne Little League complex was built decades ago, during a time when community revolved around America's pastime. Stripes of red, white and blue paint adorn every single concrete building inside the gated complex. The American rainbow stretches from the first base stands, across the dugouts, press box and snack shop, completing its patriotic journey as it adorns the league offices and third base stands.

It is also home to the best field in all of town. No doubt, it's the best field any of the boys ever laid eyes on. And from what they can tell on TV, it's better than Shea or Yankee stadium. That, of course, is in their not-so-humble opinion. The Little League also has one thing no place in town had for kids: lights! And lights mean night games! Just like the pros on TV. Heck, even Wrigley Field doesn't play night games yet. Other superb attributes of this baseball mecca include a top-notch snack stand (churros for days on end) and a ticket giveaway for a free soda or snack if you return a foul ball to the press box.

Located towards the western end of First Street in the shadow of the Bayonne Bridge, it is literally a beacon of light on a summer night. Being nestled among the darkness of the surrounding park, the Bridge and the abandoned refinery, no other place nearby has lights on at night.

The complex is absolute heaven for Jimmy and the boys. Best of all? About an eight-minute walk from Jimmy's house. Quicker if you hustle. He can even hear the press box announcements as he steps out of his house. On the approach to the front gate, the scoreboard comes into full view. Anticipation builds along the walk to the stadium; who's playing tonight? And more importantly, who's winning? Every night, all summer long the complex bustles with activity and excitement for the evening games. Walking through the front gate always brings a smile to Jimmy's face.

A home away from home. Freedom to roam. To play. To build friendships and to simply play ball. What more could a kid possibly ask for?

Night after night, Jimmy enjoys the friendly confines of Bayonne Little League. Whether he is playing in the game on the field or the one outside it. Whether solo or with the boys. Not a care in the world. Armed with just an old tennis ball and a glove. Baseballs, of course, are only allowed on the field of play itself.

The freedom of youth. *His* youth.

Jimmy's nightly routine revolves around his glove, that beat-up tennis ball and the concrete stands housing the parents. The cinder block retaining wall supporting the twenty-foot high twin structures on each baseline provide the perfect red, white and blue canvas for creating an array of childhood games with boundless configurations.

Those contests mostly consist of his own imaginary baseball game. On evenings when the boys aren't around, Jimmy simply assumes the roll of pitcher, infielder and outfielder and plays his own "Perfect Game". The repeating "thwack" of the tennis ball meeting cinder block a siren sound for his imagination at play.

One late July evening, in the middle of another solo fictional no-hit masterpiece, the freshly painted blue door to the league offices cracks open, and out steps Mr. Bexton. The musty, smoke-filled room is discreetly situated between the third base dugout and the snack-stand. The offices operate essentially as a clubhouse for the "elders," the old men responsible for operating the league and creating all of the rules. Mr. Bexton is a chief elder around these parts and certainly one very much in favor of enforcing the rules.

Initially, Jimmy doesn't pay much mind to him, although he does his best to steer clear of the guy. Hoping Mr. Bexton doesn't notice him playing ball. Praying he doesn't.

None of the kids like Mr. Bexton. And in fact, he likes the kids even less. Ironic for a senior official of a Little League, but that's not something anyone can do anything about. Mean. Old. Nasty. And those are the more glowing compliments kids extend dear Mr. Bexton. The boys are far more creative when in their own company.

Upon exiting the office, the curmudgeon squints towards the third base stands, noticing Jimmy playing ball. The boy repeatedly firing his tennis ball against the cinder block wall. Playing baseball, or really anything for that matter, is a practice he absolutely deplores inside the facility.

Prayers unanswered. And no, the irony of Mr. Bexton's view towards children playing certainly isn't lost on a ten-year-old either.

Mr. Bexton begins approaching Jimmy with his typical slow gait. A hitch in his left hip slowing him down significantly. Grimacing in his light blue polo shirt and navy shorts. Tattered brown boat shoes and a gray flat cap hat completing the ensemble.

"What do you think you're doing?" Mr. Bexton gruffly asking Jimmy.

"Just playing ball, sir." Knowing it is squarely against his rules, but when you're caught, you're caught. Own it.

"Why do you even bother?" An odd question befuddling the young boy.

"Excuse me, sir?"

"You heard me. Why do you even bother?" Mr. Bexton bluntly repeating.

"Uh, because it's fun, sir?" Really no way to properly answer that, Jimmy surmises, so go with the obvious.

"Wiseass. Didn't you hear what I told you at registration?"

Wiseass? That was an honest comment. This guy really is a

jerk, Jimmy mutters under his breath.

Registration for next season took place the week before. Jimmy and Mom visited the League Offices as per protocol and went through the mechanics of signing up to play next year: birth certificate, parent's information, emergency contacts, preferred position. Dear old Mr. Bexton manages the registration process. The almighty overlord of which players will be allowed to participate the following year.

Jimmy's excitement for next season is at a pinnacle. Drinking as much milk as he could each day, hoping to hit a growth spurt over the winter and maybe, *just maybe*, be strong enough to put one over the fence for the first time. Right over the 180-foot sign in left-center field. Wouldn't that feel amazing? He could see it happening as he walks the grounds each summer night. His time is coming.

At sign-ups, Mr. Bexton mumbled something to Jimmy as Mom completed the paperwork. Jimmy didn't respond to what he said, mostly because he couldn't hear him.

"Let me tell you again. Since you must be hard of hearing. And this time you listen good."

Jimmy straightens up, not knowing what in the world is going to come next. His bony frame tightens under the blue mesh shorts and souvenir t-shirt from this past year's Orange Bowl. The shirt looks ridiculous on his scrawny frame as it's at least two sizes too big. He wears it happily anyway, an unexpected gift in the mail from his dad. Beads of sweat beginning to trickle down the back of his neck, pooling at the band-aid covering a different kind of souvenir from his last haircut.

Mr. Bexton leans down towards the boy, slowly bringing his leathery, wrinkled face three inches away. From that distance, Jimmy's able to examine his features up close and personal.

Mr. Bexton's wiry gray stubbles from days without shaving. Yellowish eyes. The disgusting white crust flapping in the corner of his chapped lips. And the smell. Ugh. The wretched gasoline smell of his breath. Jimmy knows that smell.

"I have no idea why you're even bothering. You'll never do anything in this game. No chance at all."

Jimmy freezes. Standing there stunned. Expressionless. The comment hurts. Tears welling up in his young eyes and anger in his heart. Each droplet kindling the fire burning inside of him. He is one of the better ball players in the league, what gives?

"I know your dad, boy. And you're going to be just like him. The apple doesn't fall far from the tree. That's why you're never going to amount to nothing. In baseball. In life. Nothing." Letting the words sit for a moment, Mr. Bexton then finishes his thought:

"*Fact.*"

Jimmy's blood steaming. BOILING. Mr. Bexton going for the jugular and landing a direct hit. No one hates Jimmy's father more than Jimmy. No one. And to be compared to, and even limited by, the man he so loathes hurts even more. If Mr. Bexton were one of the boys, Jimmy would clock him. The parents would have to pull him off in order to stop the beating.

Rage coursing through his veins. Yet, somehow not exploding through. Why in the world would the old man say such a thing?

In an instant, though, Jimmy checks himself. Opening his tightly clenched fists. The strain on his fingers easing. A crack of a smile appears on Mr. Bexton's decrepit face.

Gotcha, kid. Mission accomplished.

Jimmy can't retaliate. Nope, this man is a senior person in the Little League. He could squash that dream of hitting his first home run next year in an instant. He would have to let this sit. Smile back and take it. Eat the whole shit sandwich.

"Never forget that, boy. Never. Keep playing ball all you want, but you're not going anywhere but here. Get used to that."

Jimmy biting his tongue. Tasting blood. Telling himself to let it pass.

Following his final verbal jolt, Mr. Bexton begins walking back towards the snack stand. On his way happily shaking hands and greeting a few of the parents and other elders. Jimmy stands there. Stunned. Shaken. Furious.

And silent. Accepting the hateful words directed towards him.

Once distant enough away, Mr. Bexton stops, turning around to witness Jimmy still standing there. Staring blankly back at him. No longer cheerfully throwing his tennis ball and playing his imaginary "Perfect Game".

Mr. Bexton tips his cap and smiles. Savoring his victory. Smugly enjoying the boy's pain.

A moment later, following a few rather profane words under his breath, Jimmy finally calms down enough to think about what to do next. But what's an outraged ten-year-old supposed to do? Judiciously ticking through his thoughts.

Tell Mom? Nope. She would go nuclear on the place. And that would hurt his chances of playing next year. Mr. Bexton has him cornered there. Plus, Mom has enough to worry about.

Leave? Run home? No shot. Jimmy's not leaving because of him. I'll stand here all night just to show that prick how tough I am. Go ahead. Smile away, jerk.

Tell the boys? And how exactly would that go? "Oh, hey guys, before we start our game today can I talk about how Mr. Bexton hurt my feelings? He said something really mean to me."

That image is laughable.

Although, is it really that laughable? Come to think of it, the boys would probably make the best point of all. And just call it as they see it. Yup, that's exactly what they would do, and they would probably be right. "Eff that guy. That old bag has one foot in grave anyway. Just prove him wrong. Prove them all wrong." That's what they would say.

Sage advice from the crew.

That's how it's done. No need to talk to anyone. Decision made. Screw that guy. Screw everyone. Time to prove them all wrong. Mr. Bexton, my dad, whoever comes my way.

Thanks boys. I owe you one.

Armed with this internal battle stance, Jimmy grabs his tennis ball and glove, stares intently at the cinder block stands, and proceeds to relentlessly fire that yellow sphere against the dense retaining wall for the next ten minutes. As hard as he possibly can. Over and over.

They're not going to stop me.

Jimmy pushes the tennis ball to its elastic limits with each furious pitch against the wall. Finishing once and for all after expending all of the emotion of the moment— his shoulder throbbing, fingers tingling with numbness. "Eff him. Eff this place. I'm getting out here. No matter what."

That was it. His mind made up. Jimmy now knows exactly what he doesn't want, or at the very least, where he doesn't want to be. Who he doesn't want to be already decided well before tonight.

Not My Father's Son

—————

7

The next morning, the boys gather again at the Pony League field, spending another hot summer day playing their version of sandlot baseball. The smell of freshly cut grass greeting their arrival at the diamond.

Thanks, Biscuits. Good looking out.

Fluid summer schedules mean attendance varies day-by-day, so the rules of the game are flexible. Today, eight players in total. Of course, playing four-on-four baseball presents its own unique set of challenges, but the boys never seem to mind. Simplify the game: batters are required to only pull the ball and all outs are registered at the pitcher's mound. Positions rotate. No walks allowed, swing the bat or don't bother to play. Each game lasts six innings, then the boys pick new teams. The rules resemble an odd cousin of the pick-up basketball games they play at the courts in the wintertime.

In addition to his bat and beaten-up Rawlings glove, Jimmy carries something else with him today. A chip on his shoulder. A big friggin' chip, seemingly weighing nearly half as much as he does. Perhaps more. He is getting out of this place. And ball is going to help him do it.

"Eff them all. No one is getting in my way."

As fate would have it, today just so happens to be his turn for the daily ragging. Chips tend to attract that kind of attention, veritable magnets for negativity.

Jimmy's ornery mood serving like chum for the sharks. The slightest comment from any of the boys just stoking his internal fire. Comment by comment forcefully landing another log onto the flame. The inferno burning brighter. Any remark about his game is especially grating. Because today, Mr. Bexton is the coach inside his head. And Jimmy can't shake him. Can't prove him wrong.

Stepping to the plate in the first, his back foot a twisting cork-screw, coiling as he prepares to strike. "Why do you even bother?" the inner voice calls as the pitch is delivered. Ping. A gentle pop fly that Big Smooth catches behind his back. Displaying how easy it is to put Jimmy back on the bench. Broomstick starting in. "WHOA. Crushed that one. You on fire today boy! It almost made it out of the infield. Maybe we should get a pink bouncy ball so you could hit farther?"

"Yeah, I'm on fire today," Jimmy mumbles to himself, head down, returning to the shade of the dugout.

The next inning, a close play in the field, Jaws racing to first on a routine ground ball to Jimmy playing shortstop. "Out." "Safe." "Out." "Safe." The teams siding with Jaws, he's safe at first. "You'll never do anything in this game." The surly critic within reminds him. Jimmy will just have to throw it harder next time. Jaws gloats while dancing an awkward jig on first base. "I've seen better arms on a chair. A broken chair. In a dumpster fire."

Or maybe next time Jimmy will just throw the ball *at* Jaws.

A slow grounder to Jimmy's right two batters later. Quickly shuffling his feet to the spot only as he gets there, somehow the ball rolls under his glove. That's always such an easy play for him. Always...until today. "HA! No chance at all." Mr. Bexton's wicked smile flashes to his mind.

Casanova seizes an opportunity to pour on further. "Dude, my grandmother could have reached that ball. And she's dead." Each remark passing judgement. Though firmly rooted in jest, reopening the still raw wounds from Mr. Bexton. Maybe that old bag is right? Jimmy begins to react to the comments, hurling a few generous curses towards his friend's way. "Eff off. You only made your team because your brother is on it. You know you suck."

Blood in the water. A violation of rule number two. Jimmy is taking it personal.

Can the boys get him to snap? They salivate upon seeing Jimmy react; cracking him now becomes more of a sport than the actual game. They all know exactly when they have their hooks in. No delineation of team, everyone against one from here on out. The race is on to find out who can deliver the knockout blow.

It's an odd way to treat friends for sure, but the deeper meaning stands true. Each of the boys knows that in order to get out of this town you have to be tough. Damn tough. This unspoken bond between friends is there to make sure they are all strong enough to take it. And to keep moving forward. Understand when to act and how to react.

The sharks start to circle.

Jimmy steps to the plate. Distracted and annoyed. He really is playing terribly today. And the worse he plays, the more the anger builds. His internal thermometer eclipsing the blazing summer sun overhead. The voice inside his head with one final dagger as Jimmy grabs the dented twenty-nine-inch Easton Black Magic resting against the dugout fence. His turn to bat.

"I know your dad, boy. The apple doesn't fall far from the tree."

He digs into the batter's box. Determined to crush whatever comes his way. It's time to shut everyone up. Time to prove them wrong. To quiet the voice inside his head forever. A meatball pitch served right over the heart of the plate. Oh man, this is it. His eyes lighting up, the laces are spinning right into his sweet spot…

Doink. A weak dribbler foul down the third base line.

Kermit keels over laughing on the pitcher's mound. Time to go for the kill shot. "Hey, yo. Your dad teach you to hit like that? F'n wuss."

Jimmy never says a word. The raging bull only seeing red. The black Easton hurling through the air like a helicopter blade, spinning top speed as it narrowly misses Kermit's head. Immediately after, Jimmy charges towards the mound, the volcano inside erupting uncontrollably. Kermit drops his glove to the grass. Ready to fight.

Fists clamping and punches thrown. No one intervening. The boys don't dare. Someone starts it. Someone has to end it. A flurry of fists, uppercuts and haymakers. All heads shots both ways. This isn't boxing. It's a street fight between friends on a pitcher's mound. Scratch, claw, punch, kick, do whatever you have to do to win. Make no mistake though, winning is all about the knockout. Fury. Rage. A day's worth of anger boils to the surface in a spastic windmill of punches.

Jimmy lands a few strong rights to the side of Kermit's head, though not enough to overpower him. Neither boy able to pull the other to the ground. The fight continues a few more minutes. Ending as Kermit lands a right hook while Jimmy's head is down.

BANG! Jimmy's left eye cut. Swollen. The fight is over. "Now get your punk ass off the field. Go on." Kermit shoves Jimmy to ground as Jimmy covers his eye.

Neither boy shedding a tear despite the bruises. The punch stings, but his pride hurts more. Jimmy knows he's done for the day. The rules of engagement clearly establish what happens to the offending party next: violate either rule, and you're gone. No need for that nonsense here. Go cool off somewhere and maybe we'll see you tomorrow.

Banishment.

Go toughen up and learn how to take a joke. Not exactly in the condition to go home and face Mom; his explanation for the knot engulfing his left eye not coalescing just yet. Instead, Jimmy decides to take a walk and "cool off".

Grabbing his glove and hurriedly exiting the field through the gate by first base. Leaving his bat behind in the grass out by second base, too embarrassed to make the walk to retrieve it. Once through the gate, Jimmy turns right and takes the path behind the field. The stretch of black asphalt will take him near the waterway and lead towards the Little League field. Jimmy huffs and puffs the remaining bits of anger out as he walks with his head down. Sulking and brooding with each step. Too humiliated to make eye contact with any of the boys as he completes the walk of shame past the field.

Quickly approaching a split in the path on the backside of the Little League. Finally glancing up, the imposing steel arches of the Bayonne Bridge coming into view. Instinctively choosing the path to left, the one nearest the water. It looks open, thankfully no one around to bother him. He can head down to the water and skip some rocks, clearing some space for him to think about today's events. And maybe even last night too. Thirty yards or so onto the path, Jimmy is fixing his mind on how many rocks it would take to skip in order to feel better.

"That's a pretty interesting way to treat your friends," comes a voice close by. Soft, but sturdy enough to be heard loud and clear.

"Say what?" Visibly annoyed from thinking no one else was on this path, Jimmy turns to see a man sitting on a bench facing the water reading what appears to be an old book. He surmises it's old because it has a leather cover. Jimmy only sees books like that in his grandparents' house. He immediately recognizes the man from the neighborhood.

Yup. Should have known. Only he couldn't see the bench from the fork in the path, as it's hidden carefully behind a giant fir tree. Ugh. The old guy that just sits in the park reading all the time? Today keeps getting worse.

Carpenter Joe is old by relative terms for a ten-year old. He is tall, clearing six-feet foot easily. An athletic and muscular frame with the jaw to match. The powerful hands of a carpenter gently clutching his book. Closing the cover as Jimmy draws closer. He's dressed well for a hot summer day. Light tan pants and a white polo shirt. Shoes with no socks and a linen newsboy cap covering his mildly salt and pepper hair. Hazel eyes and a soft smile. Jimmy notices he is dressed like Mr. Bexton, but the similarities end quickly thereafter. Despite the heat, Carpenter Joe looks comfortable, even at ease, with the stifling humidity. It's hard to notice if he's even sweating.

"I really don't need a speech from one of the neighborhood nice guys right now," Jimmy thinks to himself.

"Did you hear me, kid? That's an interesting way to treat your friends."

"What's it to you?" Jimmy petulantly responding. The chip, while knocked loose by Kermit, still resting firmly on his shoulder.

"You keep that nonsense up, and you won't have many friends left, if at all."

"Oh, you saw what happened from all the way over here? You superman or something?"

"Seeing is overrated. I prefer to listen."

"Who cares? See, hear, whatever. I don't need them anyway. I'm getting out of here."

Jimmy starts walking away. Disgruntled that his vision of skipping rocks in the water is rudely interrupted. Only he didn't walk away alone, Carpenter Joe stands and joins him. Not invited, nor did he ask to be. "And why are you looking to leave?" he asks the boy.

"Because. I'm not going to get stuck here. I'm out."

"Is that so? Good for you then. Do you have any idea where you're going?"

"Not here."

"Ah, sounds like a nice place. Where is that, exactly?"

"Why are you giving me a problem too?"

"Fair enough." Carpenter Joe holds both hands up, signifying no danger in his words. "I don't want to give you a problem, in fact I'd prefer to help if I could. So how about I just listen? No more questions, promise."

Jimmy looks right into Carpenter Joe's eyes, sizing him up. Squinting his eyes and scanning him head to toe. Is this guy for real?

Jimmy's eyes soften after the momentary scan. His guard eases, his gut sensing something good about Carpenter Joe. Enough of a sense at least to give him a chance. There's something familiar about him. Jimmy sees him around, sure, but they never really talked other than a "hello" or something like that. He offers the boys some baseball pointers every now and then, which Jimmy thinks is cool. The guy knows what he's talking about. When it comes to baseball at least.

Being one of the nice guys also means he isn't one of the neighborhood creepers. Jimmy is absolutely sure of that. Just as the boys know who the nice guys are, they keep tabs on the creepers too, warning each other who to stay away from. The creepers like spending time around kids too. Just in ways they make after school specials about.

For some reason, Jimmy senses this guy *cares*. And honestly, it feels weird at first. There's another feeling that comes after the caring though. It's not one he experiences much with adults, particularly men.

Trust. Unconscious of how to define it at first.

Jimmy overcomes the initial hesitancy. A mildly deep breath accompanies the release of his angst. And so, the two of them begin to walk the first few steps of the path together. After all, today can't get any worse, can it?

Ten or twelve yards further on, Jimmy opens the floodgates. Out of nowhere the boy starts talking…and talking…and talking. More than he ever has in his entire life.

And Carpenter Joe beside him listening. Keeping his promise. Confirming Jimmy's gut instinct.

Jimmy filling him in on life. All of it. For the first time in his life someone offering to listen. And then actually did listen. How much he loves baseball with the boys, even with something like today happening. "It's awesome being on the field with them. We have the whole place to ourselves and we just get to do our own thing out there. Sure, we get on each other sometimes, but that doesn't mean anything. They're my friends."

Jimmy explains the ribbings between them are referred to as "crack fights". As in cracking jokes on one another. Unfortunately, sometimes that leads to trying to crack each other's skulls. They are never meant to be personal. Today, he took them personal.

He rolls on from one version of family to another.

Bryan. An incredible older brother. They might not talk much, but Jimmy always knows they're on the same page. And Bryan looks out for him. "The guy is amazing. Not a bad bone in his body. He teaches me a lot of stuff, but he's also cool with me being me. Never tries to push me into anything I don't want to do. Or force me to copy him. I appreciate that."

Mom. An elementary school nurse in neighboring Jersey City. Spending this summer working three jobs because Dad refuses to pay child support. They have to keep their house, and it's the only way. Mom doesn't talk much. About anything. She works hard and keeps up a good image for her boys. She cries, though, a lot, mostly spending time at the kitchen counter sobbing. Mom used to smoke, but thankfully recently stopped cold turkey. "She tells us life is really hard. To fight and do whatever we can to not end up like her. I get that, sort of. I know Mom gives us everything she can every day. It's not a lot compared to other people, but you know she wants us to know the good things about life."

Dad. Two memories stand out most. The one time he burned him with cigarettes all afternoon because he played dressed up in his father's shoes, sunglasses, overcoat and hat. "I was just playing around one Saturday when I was a little kid. It was only me and him at home. Thought it would be fun, so I put on his tan raincoat and big blue sunglasses. Danced around in his smelly leather shoes. Man, he *hated* that. Told me to shut my mouth, sit on the floor next to his chair and hold his beer. Rest of the day, he burned me on the head with a bunch of cigarettes like I was his ashtray or something. Told me he did it there so Mom couldn't see the marks under my hair. The burns stopped hurting after a while, but I still remember that smell." Jimmy unconsciously rubbing his head while recalling the time with his father. Some scars taking more time to heal than others.

"Dad took it personal. It wasn't meant to be personal."

And the day Dad left. Easter Sunday a few years ago. Mom and Dad fighting all morning. "Finally, Dad stood up from the dining room table, stepped over me as I was playing on the floor with the Matchbox cars I got from the Easter Bunny and walked out the front door. Mom just put her head down on the table and cried for a while." Jimmy's eyes watering reliving the moment in time. Though careful not to let Carpenter Joe see tears coming out.

"Dad never came back. And he never said goodbye."

Jimmy elaborating on his father a bit more for Carpenter Joe. Explaining that Dad was a "drinker". At least that's what Jimmy knew of him, or, rather, what Mom told of him. Carpenter Joe kept listening as they continue walking side by side, Carpenter Joe on the left, Jimmy on his right-hand side. From the moment he promised, the older of the two remained silent. Never speaking a word, instead keeping his word.

Jimmy then telling the story about Mr. Bexton. About what he said. How much it hurt. How he knew it wasn't true. How he *hoped* it wasn't true.

"Do you mind if I ask a question now?" Carpenter Joe requesting permission to speak.

"Sure, I guess it's okay."

"Do you believe it to be true?"

Jimmy a bit taken back. Not really understanding the question. "Believe what to be true?"

"What that man said. About the apple tree. And you. Do you believe that to be true?"

"I dunno. Maybe. Everybody says it for a reason, right?"

"Well, what is common is not always true."

"What chu talkin' bout Carpenter Joe?" Jimmy paraphrasing one of his favorite TV characters.

"That's funny, kid. Let me explain. Take the apple tree. That's not how apples actually grow. Sure, they all come from apple seeds. Just like people come from people." Carpenter Joe continuing on, in spite of the look of utter confusion plastered on Jimmy's sunburned face. "Listen closely, the seeds from the apple that fell are entirely unique and do not produce the same exact apple as the parent. In fact, the apple that falls *must* be paired with seeds of another. And together they create their own tree, able to produce all kinds of apples. Go ahead, think of your brother. You both share the same blood as your Dad, but you are all not one in the same. You each stand alone. Each free to choose where you go in this world so you can grow your own tree."

Jimmy's mind working in overdrive attempting to discern the lesson. What is this guy *getting* at?

"Allow me to explain it another way. The knowledge inside the seeds dictate that as they grow, they must become an apple. However, what *kind* of apple the seeds grow into depends on what happens *after* it falls."

Jimmy stops striding forward, instead standing in awe. Mouth agape. Never before hearing such a thing. Not in any text-book or church sermon. A look of concern appears on Jimmy's sunburned face. Understanding the concept, just doubting the truth held within it. "I'm following. Just never heard anything like that before."

Gravitating to everyone he knows. Children of cops want to become cops. Children of teachers want to be teachers. Children of lawyers want to be lawyers. Contractors, doctors, carpenters, stockbrokers, firemen…on and on it goes. The cycle repeats itself. Children of drinkers become drinkers.

Now you're telling me there's a choice?

Carpenter Joe watching the boy's face light up, the fog of

confusion lifting, Jimmy's eyes twinkling with excitement regarding his discovery of the truth about apples. And about himself. "So, the apple *can* fall far from the tree? I don't have to follow anyone's footsteps?"

"The apple *did* fall from the tree. How far depends on the steps taken after that, the ones *you* take. How you live your life is a choice. Much like you chose to take this particular path and walk by me on the bench."

"So, this means that old fart Mr. Bexton really doesn't know what he's talking about, right?" Joe quickly responds, "Unfortunately, farts stink, kid. Some more than others. Remember the lesson, though. It's not whether Mr. Bexton is right or wrong; it's what *you* know to be true.

The merry-go-round in his mind slowly bringing itself to halt. Jimmy grasping the teachings at hand. Carpenter Joe remains on point as he sees Jimmy decode the lesson. "Unfortunately, many don't ever realize that. They *believe* the apple doesn't fall far from the tree. So, the tree is all they see, never bothering to look around at all the other possibilities in their life."

"I think I get it. But how do you know? How do you look past the tree?" An ever-grateful smile appearing on Carpenter Joe's face: "Excellent question. Look around you. What do you see?"

Jimmy pauses again on the path, surveying the park and their surroundings, trying to see whatever it is his companion sees. "The park?" A feeble answer if there ever was one. But at least it's an answer.

"True, yes. But how will you get back to your mom's house?"

Jimmy scans the grounds again. The path right, the path left, racing across the grass to cross from one path over to the other, scaling a fence to take a shortcut through Little League, the hidden back gate at the Pony League field. There are endless possibilities! Jimmy's face brightening as he calculates the potential avenues to take back to Mom's house.

Carpenter Joe notices the subtle shift taking place. "Amazing what happens when you change the way you look at what's right in front of you, isn't it?"

"Yeah! Wow. I think I could take a million different ways! But how do I know which one is the right one?" Jimmy growing brighter still at the potential adventures before him.

"Look again."

Another examination of the environment. Jimmy sees the paths twist and turn, none of them straight. Some that are closer to the water than others. Some drift further away. Other paths concealed in the shadows, their foundations cracked from the harsh elements of Jersey winters. Still others, smooth, perhaps recently resurfaced, bathing in the summer sun. "I'm still not sure which one is the right one," Jimmy cautiously responds, dimming ever so slightly.

"Looking beyond the tree means seeing all that is possibile. The path you take from there is the one *you choose*. Each offering something different to the traveler. And no matter which path you walk, they all lead to the same place."

"Where's that?"

"Home."

Squinting his eyes, Jimmy views the park as if transported there for the very first time in his young life. Playing each course out in his mind's eye, astonished that Carpenter Joe is right. He's right! No matter which way I go, I can still go home. Which way is *my choice*. A slight smile appears on Carpenter Joe's face. Today's lesson appears complete.

"Mind if I ask you a question, sir?" Jimmy asking somewhat awkwardly.

"Of course, kid. Go ahead."

"Are you a farmer or something? Is that book an almanac? I can't figure out why you know so much about apples and seeds living in Bayonne. Hanging in this park all the time."

"HA!" Carpenter Joe belly laughs at the notion. Then, he considers it for a moment. The boy does have a point. "Sure, kid. You can think of me as a farmer. And this book speaks about how to plant seeds and help them grow."

"A book about seeds, huh? Really interesting stuff there Old MacDonald," Jimmy says with a wry smile. Feeling lighter than air after learning the truth about apple trees.

"Okay, wise guy. It's best you pick your path for today and go take care of that eye. I imagine your mom will love the story about that one."

"Shoot. I forgot. You're right, I gotta go. Alright then, Old MacDonald. See you around the farm." Jimmy bounces off, smiling.

"See ya around, kid."

Jimmy freezes seemingly mid-bounce. "Sorry, one more question. You're Carpenter Joe, right?"

"Just Joe, kid. And you are?"

"Jameson. My friends call me Jimmy, though."

"Jameson, huh?"

"Told you my dad was a drinker. I guess he wanted to make sure the apple didn't fall too far from the tree." Laughing at the notion in light of today's lesson.

Joe laughs along with the young boy. "Well, it's a pleasure to meet you Jimmy. You know, it seems to me when the apple tree is removed it's a lot easier for the apple to see how big the orchard is."

Jimmy smiles gently at the analogy. "I get it."

"Say, will you do me one favor the next time you're over at the Little League?"

"Sure thing, Joe. You want a churro or something?"

Grinning while he answers, Joe responds, "Be sure to thank Mr. Bexton the next time you see him. And yes, a churro would be nice."

"HUH?!? *Thank* that grumpy old bat? For what?" Clearly the most confusing thing Jimmy has heard all day.

"Perhaps he is worth looking at a little differently as well. Because without him, you don't choose this path today. And you don't learn the truth about apple trees. In time, you may discover that we're all part of each other's paths, even people like Mr. Bexton."

Huh, indeed. One final lesson for the day. "Okay, then. I'll thank that old b...fogey, how about old fogey? I'm sure he'll really get a kick out of that. And two churros for us coming up. Can I find you here?"

"Fogey is good start. And you can find me wherever you need to on these paths."

The two new friends parting ways at a fork near the bench where their journey first began. Joe returning to his seat facing the water. Jimmy surveying the interlacing asphalt trails again, choosing an unconventional path home. On the surface, the two appear to be an odd couple. But underneath the unusual outward appearance, lay the foundation for a lifelong friendship.

One that will certainly be tested. One question standing above the others: how will the lessons of youth stand up against the rigors of time?

A View of the Orchard

8

THE NOONDAY SUN OF THE PRESENT DAY NOW SHINING BRIGHTLY OVERHEAD, REMOVING THE MORNING CHILL FROM THE AIR. WARM ENOUGH FOR JIMMY TO OPEN HIS JACKET AND LET THE BREEZE OFF THE WATER PROVIDE SOME RELIEF FROM THE HEAT OF THE CONVERSATION.

Collins Park fills with more patrons: dog walkers, runners, bike riders and skate boarders. All out enjoying the sunshine of a Fall afternoon.

"You remember, now, don't you?" Joe says to the boy, now the grown man standing before him.

"I do. I remember that. That was a looong time ago, though. Why bother to bring it up now?"

"Come on, kid, would you really like me to spell it out for you?" Joe only modestly joking.

"No, no. Fine. I get it. I had a choice then and I have a choice now. I always have a choice."

"About what?"

"About what path to take. About how I want to live life."

"Exactly. Well, would you look at that. It's good to see some lessons have staying power. Although, that's only part of the truth."

"Ha. Ha. I get the point, Old MacDonald."

A gentle laugh from Joe. "Oh, is that it? Would you like me to sing about all the animals on my farm?" Jimmy smirks. "No need. I know that you're a heck of a farmer. But I doubt you're a great singer, too."

"Fair enough, kid. So, *you* made the choice of a big change, a transformation if you will. A choice to change course, follow a different path. Perhaps there is something else you found along the way?"

Jimmy lets out a deep sigh. "I'm not so sure I found anything. Everything seemed easier, even just a few months ago, even on the path to making the change. Just more straightforward." Jimmy continues, explaining in further detail, "We have kids, a family to take care of. I don't want to disappoint them. Disappoint Quinn."

"That's nothing new. You were married to Quinn and had kids as you went down this path. Living your choice."

"I don't know about that Joe. This is the version of me they know, the only one my kids know anyway. I don't what to screw up what they know."

Joe counters, "What about *who* they know?" Jimmy shakes his head at the notion, an audible exhale accompanying the gesture. "It's not that. Really. At least I don't think it is."

"So, they know who you are?"

"Ugh. Come on. Enough already. That's not it, I'm telling you. My job as a dad was, or is, to teach them about hard work. Sacrifice. To show them what that looks like so they can make a good living someday."

"And who will teach them about how to make a life?" Jimmy

huffs at Joe's response. No words come out following his exhale. Joe presses on, open to see where the answers lead. "Family isn't what's holding you back, and since that's not it, what is?"

Jimmy offers a flustered response to Joe's questions. "I don't want anything to go wrong. But I just don't know what's going to happen."

Joe rocks his head back upon hearing Jimmy's response. "And you did before?" Accentuating the interrogative.

"I guess, yeah, before the change anyway. Life was straight-forward. Go to work. Get paid. Then get to do stuff you want to do. Family time, vacation, enjoy life, whatever."

"Sounds invigorating." Joe dryly pointing out the obvious.

"I didn't say it was exciting. At times it was, yes. But I knew what to expect and knew how to handle all of it. So long as I did what I was supposed to do, then I get what I wanted out of life outside of work. It was all laid out in front of me."

Joe parrots back the key phrases in Jimmy's answer: "What to expect...what to do...what I want..."

"That's not my point. It was safe. Secure."

"*Certain*? Is that it?

"Yeah, that's it. I was certain of what was going to happen. I could plan."

"Oh, so that's what you were truly seeking all this time? Certainty?"

"Yes." Jimmy says frustratingly.

"Appears we found your definition of success."

Jimmy's frustration escalating, "I worked my ass off for nearly twenty years for that certainty. I earned it."

"So, all that time you were making something of yourself, all those experiences in life, whether they be a long-distance rela-tionship into a marriage, being told no children into a father times four, the light and dark side of the corporate ladder. Through all of that, you just kept filling your cup up with certainty, blissfully drinking away the fear of the unknown. Is that it?"

Jimmy stops walking, noticeably annoyed at another reframing of his life. "I fought hard for certainty, Joe."

"Keep fighting. You'll find it at the end."

"What?" Jimmy instantly moving from frustrated to visibly agitated.

"Kid, there are three certainties for every man, woman and child on this Earth. How it begins. How it ends. And that everything in between is uncertain." Joe takes a moment before continuing. "Allow me to modify my original question then. *Who* is the one holding you back? Because it's rather clear from where I'm standing."

"What?!" Jimmy apoplectic at the implication. Agitated moving to livid.

"I said, who." Joe responds calmly, not raising his voice in the slightest. "Sowing seeds of certainty is like believing apples don't fall far from the tree. They both breed fear of the possible."

"What do you know? You're still walking around this crappy little park. Sitting there on your bench reading the same book over and over again. Sounds pretty damn certain to me." Immediately, Jimmy regrets the harsh tone, but stands his ground. Wanting to take Joe to task. The student finally pushing to turn the inquisition around after all these years. Seemingly having enough of the one-sided "conversations."

Joe barely engages the comment. Instead, simply letting it roll off him, brushing it away as if it were a buzzing gnat. Shoo-fly, don't bother me. "I am in this park because I choose to be. I was not certain of who I would meet today or what I would learn. However, I was certain of who I would *be* today, and after that, I am open to all that is possible on this path." Joe tilts his head forward, engaging eye to eye with Jimmy.

"And you? Is there something you wished to learn? Or perhaps someone you intended to meet?"

Just like that, any hope of turning the tide against Joe vanishes. Jimmy just left staring at Joe's raised eyebrows and wrinkled forehead, looking back at him awaiting an answer. Silence the only response provided.

Joe begins walking, Jimmy trailing slight behind. "Let's proceed further. Since you recall our conversation about the apple tree, then perhaps it's time to consider what's *inside* the apple." Joe allows the pivotal word to slowly and intentionally drift towards its target. He then immediately continues once the word lands, not letting the sideways nature of the conversation deter him any longer from continuing today's lesson. "And you lived closer to this topic, certainty and uncertainty, than most often do. The lesson that is rooted at the core of experiencing Life. That I can assure you."

Carpenter Joe is not giving in. There is more here to learn. That Jimmy *must* learn. His hazel eyes stare Jimmy down like never before. Peering straight into his soul. Is he looking for the boy he once knew?

Jimmy pauses again on the old familiar path, anxiously trying to figure out Joe's next move, cowering slightly from Joe's intense gaze. Zero clue what to expect, even after so much time together. Perhaps the years apart changing them both.

Then, Joe does something peculiar. Bizarre, even. He starts *singing*. An absurdly poorly executed deep baritone…

"Pretty Woman, walking down the street….Pretty Woman… the kind I'd like to meet…."

Instantly Jimmy's shoulders slouch forward. Eyes roll in the back of his head, then close tightly. He knows. No other song in the world could conjure up such memories as that one. "Oh, man. That friggin guy?" Jimmy's body waives the white flag of surrender before Joe could sing another part of the refrain. Joe acknowledges the yielding of verbal arms yet continues to hum the melody. Bum, bum, bum…bum…

"Yes, kid. ***That*** guy."

SECTION THREE

The Wall Between

Who the Hell Lives Next Door?

9

1989 IS ANOTHER SWELTERING HOT SUMMER IN BAYONNE. RECORD LEVELS OF HEAT AND HUMIDITY DAILY. THE UNRELENTING SUN MAGNIFYING THE ENERGY OF THE BOYS, EMBOLDENING THEM. THEY NOW REIGN SUPREME AS KINGS OF THE NEIGHBORHOOD.

Endless summer days and nights of baseball and laughter, with the occasional mischievous adventure and street fight mixed in. Exploring and trespassing are strange bedfellows when you roll as part of the downtown crew. Fences are meant to be climbed, anyways.

Another year of childhood means growing taller, stronger and more confident. For Jimmy, that means in who he is, who he wants to be and where he wants to go. Ever grateful for an understanding about apple trees and open orchards.

The summer of '89 is a blast. Of course, until someone comes along and messes it all up.

About a year or so after Joe and Jimmy spoke about apple trees and choosing a path, another mysterious person appears in his life. Only he isn't another elder from the Little League, a coach or a priest from church. Nor is he from some far-away place and new to town. Sometimes trouble simply comes knocking from the places you least expect it.

Funny how that works, isn't it? Just as the rains of some great tempest in life pass, another storm emerges. Ever larger. Potentially more challenging. Ominous. Mr. Bexton and even the imagery of Jimmy's own father pale in comparison to what, or rather *who*, emerges in life's next chapter.

The boy is happily unaware of a threat on the horizon as he sits on the concrete steps outside Mom's house each morning lacing up his sneakers. After all, this is summer.

Each of the brick faced townhomes on First Street are small, quaint, with a set of nine concrete steps leading up to the front door. No front yard, a small spit of land in the back, enough for a deck or a patch of grass. Jimmy's house shares a stairway with their neighbor to the left. A single white painted wrought iron railing the dividing line between the properties. Two of the other townhomes have a similar property line between them.

The most distinguishing feature about Jimmy's house is that is has a deck off the dining room on the first floor, the only one with that luxury on the row. That compensates for the lack of side yard that the homes on each end enjoy. The family makes the small house work these days. It's big enough for everyone, at least while the boys are still small enough, anyways. Of course, it helps having Collins Park across the street. In Jimmy's mind, it's still the best, and biggest, front yard in all of Bayonne.

The five-block radius of the downtown neighborhood surrounding Jimmy's home operates as a protected zone, his sanctuary. So long as he continues to stay in that contained area, Mom is fine with him going anywhere he chooses. Casanova's house on Fifth Street is the northern border. The Little League complex the western border and the basketball courts across the from the neighboring yellow-tinted housing projects the eastern border. Collins Park and the Kill Van Kull waterway serving as the natural southern boundary.

Most importantly, it's safe. The neighborhood nice guys are still on watch. Biscuits manicuring the field, Chops manicuring their hair and Salty dutifully serving up the lone item on his menu. And, for the most part, the boys stay out of trouble…for the most part.

On this mid-summer day, Jimmy follows his long-standing summer routine. Ball during the day, break for dinner, then meet the boys at the Little League for the evening's festivities. Tonight is a little different than usual, though, at least for the rest of the family. Mom is out with her friends, and Bryan, tasting his first bite of teenage freedom, is throwing a party at the house. Simple enough. A small gathering. The plan for everyone to be out well before Mom is due home.

Well, it doesn't take an advanced degree to understand what happens to teenage party plans. True to form, some older friends, naturally not all on the original invite list, manage to secure a dozen or so cases of beer and take it upon themselves to open the invitation.

Or, more accurately, bust the invitation wide open. Small things grow to big things. Especially when high school freshman and sophomores are involved.

Walking back from the Little League, Jimmy hears the party in full swing upon on his approach. Not a full on rager, but loud enough for a relatively quiet neighborhood. He knows the song playing as he approaches the house, Young MC's "Bust a Move". Even allowing himself a little two-step shimmy before hitting the runway to the stairs. "Dude, you better clean that up before Mom gets home." Saying to himself as he curls left from the sidewalk, gathering speed to bounce up the stairs and inside the house. "And I'm not helping."

Hitting the fourth step, springing with enthusiasm. After all, it's his first high school party, too. From the nearby shadows, "HEY! KID! Tell your brother to shut that **GOD DAMN** music off! How dare you kids? How **DARE** you! Little bastards."

Jimmy stops dead in his tracks. Flight...fight...or freeze. Breathing heavy now, looking around, unable to see anything or anyone. Surrounded by darkness. The voice is deep, raspy, seemingly coming directly from the back of a throat, bypassing the tongue, lips and mouth entirely. Did that come from the driveway?

No.

Someone at the party hiding in the widow messing with him? Trying to scare the crap out of him? Likely. And it's working. "Jerks. See what happens if Mom comes early."

The voice again, "**HEY!** Did you hear me? You *disgusting* kids! How dare you!?"

Freezing again mid-step. Heart bursting out of his chest. This isn't a voice from one of the Bryan's friends. No one can mimic that guttural sound. The venom infused into each word. He only heard this voice a few times before. And not for a while. Though it is unmistakable now.

Oh. Damn.

Pensively looking up, glancing left over to his neighbor's house. The screen door is closed but the main door behind it is open. Frosted glass slits adorn the door in lieu of a traditional screen or clear window. The frost isn't part of the design though. It's a layer of filth and dirt covering the glass. During the day the wretched brown color is visible from across the street.

Jimmy can barely make out the shape of the person in the moonlight. No exterior light illuminates the entrance. His neighbor maintaining a constant shroud of darkness.

The lurking shadow then appears in the doorway.

Slav.

"Shit. I better tell Bryan." Jimmy doesn't acknowledge nor engage the ghastly figure as he quickly enters the house. Despite the intense glare piercing through the dirty glass door, a mere four feet away. Entering the house, he quickly navigates through the crowd. The house is packed! What in the world is Bryan thinking?!? Finally, Jimmy is able to find the host in the back-yard, holding court on the deck surrounded by four giggling teenage schoolgirls.

"Bry, we gotta talk."

"Not now man. Can you just chill somewhere until it's time to clean up?"

"Dude, no, I can't just chill. Slav is out."

"Oh, shit. You serious?"

"Yeah. Greeted me at the door. You know what he's going to do; he's going to watch everyone on the way out. Get all weird and creepy. Might call the cops, too. Guy just freaked me out."

"Damn. Eff'n Slav. I guess the party's over."

The girls frowning immediately at the suggestion, not under-standing the magnitude of what is taking place. Ignoring their disappointment, Bryan turns to the crowd, cupping his hands around his mouth in order to project over the music: "It's OVER people! Time to head out everybody. Wrap it up, and roll out."

The abruptness of it all confusing the attendees. "What gives?" the general sentiment permeating the crowd. Things are just getting going. Why mess up a good thing? Turning to his close friend Jackrabbit, Casanova's older brother, Bryan calmly explaining the situation at hand. "Look bro, it's just time to leave. Our neighbor is out. And you don't want to be around for that. Trust me man, he's bad news."

"Who the hell lives next door? Manuel Noriega? Come on man, this is just getting jumping!" Jackrabbit folding is hands in prayer, hopping in place, pleading for the festivities to continue. "Nah man. Slav. Let's just leave it at that for now. We have to clean up anyway." Jimmy shooting Bryan a confused look. "We?" Ugh.

The party ends orderly enough. A few disgruntled patrons, but nothing Bryan can't handle. One bonus of the early dismissal is that the house requires only a mild amount of cleaning.

Everything appearing to settle down well enough. The boys even managing to be done well before they expected Mom to be home. Plenty of time to relax and catch a Braves game on TV. Each boy taking their respective chill spots: Jimmy laying out on the Grandma style pink and white floral couch, Bryan on the oversized powder blue recliner. The older sibling quickly flipping around the channels to find the game.

BANG! The plaster wall dividing the homes shakes. **BANG! BANG!** The Monet impressionist print Mom hung on the wall slants sideways. Jimmy's gangly frame jumps off the couch, nervously sitting upright at the edge of the cushion. His eyes shoot open while his heart races.

"I know you two are in there!!! How dare you! How **dare** you not respect me!" The boys look at each other, both of them now stark white. What THE?!?!

BANG! BANG! The portrait box hanging next to the basement door containing Mom's knickknacks rattles. A few of the pieces falling to the navy-blue carpeted floor. Mom will certainly notice if anything breaks. Thankfully a soft landing for each piece.

"You DISGUSTING kids are going to pay for this! *PAY!!!* I swear it!!! I will get you!"

The banging and screaming continue unabated for fifteen to twenty minutes. Cursing. Yelling. The boys remain quiet. Turning the TV volume down so they could hear if Slav is moving around his house. Or moving out.

Jimmy crawls across the carpet to lock the front door, just in case. Then swiftly back to his spot, trembling ever so slightly at the unknown next door.

Both boys rattled a bit, but hyper-focused on Slav. "Let him get it all out," Bryan says, waving his hand carefree to the chaos next door, pretending not to be concerned. At that moment, the clicking sound of the garage door motor kicking on. Mom's home. Damn.

"Guess we'll have to tell her about the party," Bryan says calmly to his brother. "Yeah. Probably a good idea. At least before Slav does." The brothers laugh, assuming the worst is over.

No way he keeps this up with Mom home.

The door to the basement swings open, Mom scans the living room, assessing any potential damage from a rule's violation. The most noticeably out of place items? The boys are sitting quietly, too quietly, watching a Braves game on TV. Maternal instinct kicking in immediately. Something's up.

Another dead giveaway that something is amiss? Aside from the choir boy act? The house is spotless.

BOOM! The banging starts again. LOUDER. Fist after fist slamming heavily again and again against the thin plaster wall separating the homes. The threats continuing. NOW GROWING HARSHER.

"I'm going to kill you boys! Kill. You. When you step outside, I will kill you!"

Slav cackles as he details the sick vision in his mind. "Brryyyyaaannnn…" taunting Jimmy's older brother. Scratching the walls now instead of pounding. It's not the sound of finger-nails, could it be a knife? "Brryyyaaannnn…I am going to turn you into Bryana. You won't be a man when I'm done with you!!"

Mom's jaw drops. Covering her mouth with her left hand, using her right hand to stabilize herself against the wall near the basement door, adjacent to her knickknack window box. Slowly she sits down on the powder blue ottoman alongside to the recliner. Frozen in stunned silence. Keeping her hand up to her mouth, unsure of what, if anything, to say.

Slav's verbal assault lingers further into the night. Mom's return home did not have the outcome the boy's envisioned. "You just woke up your worst nightmare! You little pieces of shit!! I own you, and I am going slaughter you."

The brutally foul assault persists for several more minutes, which feels like an eternity for the boys. Suddenly, Mom simply stands up, walks her tiny ginger-haired five foot-two frame over to the landing at the bottom of stairs…and begins punching the wall back…screaming at the top of her lungs!

"HEY! HEY! You *shut your mouth* over there. Just shut it! Enough!"

The boys love it! Go get 'em Mom! Slav quiets down after that. Bet he never expected that response. Finally, the two townhomes on First Street are quiet for the night.

After taming the beast, Mom calmly returns to her seat on the ottoman. She doesn't speak another word until walking upstairs to retire for the night ten minutes or so later. Stopping at the landing again she looks down towards the boys.

"What did you *do*?" she said, tears streaming down her cheeks

"Nothing," Bryan answers defiantly. "We didn't *do* anything to him." Flustered by the question and assumption.

No response. Mom simply turns away, walking upstairs. The family never speaks another word about that night. The simple act of "nothing" turning into nearly a decade of war raging between neighbors. A war rarely witnessed outside those two quaint townhouses at the western end of First Street.

The boys quietly contemplating to themselves after Mom withdraws for the night. What happens now? Neither of them willing to share their true concerns with the other.

Brothers in Bayonne don't do that sort of thing.

Building Bridges and Growing Chasms

10

Slav, whose real name is Vladislav, is volatile mix of oversized troll, meandering vagrant and most notably, sociopath. He is big, easily clearing six feet, and carrying at least two hundred and ninety pounds. His rounded stomach protrudes well past his waistline. Pasty white skin, nearly translucent. Thin, greasy gray hair covers his eyes and drapes down his neck, leaving a permanent butter-like coating on the back of his shirt collar.

"Slav" seems more suitable to the brothers as a nickname than Vlad. Say it quick enough and it sounds a bit like "slob". Waddles as he walks, a balky right knee the culprit. Head always down. Never making eye contact. Constantly mumbling and wildly gesturing with his hands.

He wears the same clothes every day, regardless of the weather, blistering sun or frigid tundra. Stained white polo shirt. Light blue shorts. Calf-high thick white tube socks and generic discount shop white sneakers. A ragged navy-blue parka the only addition when the temperature drops well below freezing. Late forties, early forties is the best guess on how old he is. Hard to tell to be honest. Slav probably looks a lot older than he is.

For the next few years or so, the verbal battle between Slav and the family continues simmering, but never quite boiling over to the physical realm. His threats staying just that, threats. Each instance of Bryan hosting a party met with banging walls and a disturbing salutation from the shadow figure lurking next door as the guests leave the party.

"You should stay away from this house if you know what's good for you," Slav calls from behind his filth-covered screen door. "I own that house and those boys, too." Calling to girls leaving the party. Sickening them with his macabre commentary. "Hey young lady, you should ask Bryana how she feels to be part of the gang. I cut that kid's balls off so he could squeal like a little girl. So that he could squeal like you."

The horrifying messages become part of Slav's new routine. However, he targets them so not to be widespread amongst the patrons next door. Picking and choosing his prey as they leave the house, mostly those alone and nearly always feminine. Sowing seeds of fear from inside the darkness of his home.

Once Bryan's party ends and all the guests leave for the evening, that's when Slav's party begins. The pounding on the walls. The threats to end the boys' lives.

The viciousness becomes a sadistic ritual. But it also becomes something else…it becomes normal. So much so that they boys would go about their business cleaning the house, straightening up the furniture and removing the protective coverings on Mom's knickknacks all while being serenaded with promises of torture and mutilation.

Bryan and Jimmy joke during the verbal onslaughts about which one would receive which punishment. "You're pretty little, bro, so you're probably going to be the one that gets beaten like a dog. Maybe you're his little Shih Tzu." The boys laugh hysterically. Bryan comforting Jimmy that his penalty wouldn't be so severe.

"That's not bad, man. At least I get to go out for a walk. He already cut your balls off, so I think you're the one that gets the kitty litter box? Since you're already neutered and what not." Bryan chuckling, proudly grabbing his still attached set of chestnuts and assuring Jimmy the kitty litter box is meant for him. "Sorry bro, you get all the animal stuff. Remember man, I'm allergic, so Slav knows that's not good for me." Both brothers howl laughing as the plaster wall continually thunders.

Time passes, and the relationship between Slav, Bryan and Jimmy continually unfolds: Bryan hosts a kickass party, Slav unsettles a guest or two as they leave, then threatens the boys' lives, the boys laugh the commentary and the cleanup away.

Routine, yes. But normal? It is for Jimmy. Through it all, the time he spends with Bryan under duress becomes a highlight of his pre-teen years.

Slav doesn't cross the line, though, the physical one, anyway. The white wrought iron railing separating their shared concrete stairway serving a purpose well beyond that of a handrail. Instead it functions as a miniature demilitarized zone between Slav and the boys. Is it a barrier that will ever be crossed? Only time will tell.

During the years of this new routine, Jimmy also grows closer with his friend Joe, although their relationship operates under far different circumstances.

Finding time to be in the park is easy during the summer time. Baseball still the focal point of each day's activities. Only now, Jimmy heads down a different path when the games are over. He chooses an alternative to heading directly home, veering right at the gate on the first base side of the field, to the well-acquainted path that rounds past home plate, and onward to the Bridge.

Looking to learn something new from the old guy that sits in the park reading his book.

Turns out old Carpenter Joe played baseball when he was younger. Pretty good, too. College ball, semi-pro, even a hint at something beyond that. His dream of professional ball never fully materializing. "I played hard for as long as I could and enjoyed every minute of it. But being a baseball player is only part of who I am. Just like it's only a part of you, a piece of the whole."

As it turns out, the man who now enjoys sitting on a non-descript park bench, reading the same book in Collins Park on the banks of the Kill van Kull is a lot more worldly that one might initially suggest. Joe seemingly has been everywhere, and as they talk, Jimmy finds it nearly impossible to name a place in the world he knows about where Joe *hasn't* visited.

Big cities around the globe: London, Paris, Hong Kong, Rio de Janeiro, Tokyo, Mumbai, Sydney. "You see that bridge, kid?" pointing upwards towards the massive steel arches of the Bayonne Bridge. "Yeah. Umm…that a trick question?"

"Ha. There's a sister bridge, a twin if you will, just like it in Sydney Harbor. Beautiful place, stunning views, and amazing people."

Smaller ones in the U.S. and abroad, heck, even remote places Jimmy can't find on any map: Nashville, Worcester, Maui, Donegal, Schleiden, and some place called Mauritius. "It's an island pretty far out into the Indian Ocean. Beautiful place, stunning views, and amazing people."

Each time, Joe providing only a small hint at what brought his travels to places far and wide. "Spent some time there" is really all he ever says about the places that appear in Jimmy's mind as exotic as a trip to Mars. And after each mention of his travels, Joe ends with the same refrain, "Beautiful place, stunning views, and amazing people."

The consistency is not lost on Jimmy, however. "Joe, how

come you always say the same thing about whatever place you've been? Are they really *all* that beautiful with these A-mazing people?"

"You find what you're looking for, kid. In places and, most of all, in people. That is what I choose to find."

"Then why didn't you stay in one of *those* places? They all sound better than here."

Joe smiles. "Why? This is a beautiful place," opening his hands and spreading his arms across the landscape of Collins Park with its grass fields, playgrounds and idyllic location on the waterfront. "Stunning views," fixing his right arm upwards towards the Bridge, offering the current time and place as an example— a supertanker passing below its steel expanse. "And amazing people," bringing his gaze down from the sky back to the bench, nodding his head gently in the affirmative as looks towards Jimmy seated on his right-hand side.

Their conversations roll along like the asphalt paths of Collins Park. Twisting and turning, yet all connecting. An array of topics exposing Jimmy to the world around him. The world he is part of. This, despite rarely ever traveling past his grandparents' house on 57th Street. Subjects ranging far and wide: history, mythology, architecture, languages…

"You may hear people say something along the lines of 'learn from history, or you are doomed to repeat it'. But most times, they aren't all in agreement on what the lesson to learn is. Especially when they focus solely on the external battle."

Mythology. Fascinating stories of the relationship between the Gods, men and women. Zeus, Athena, Apollo, Neptune, Thor, Loki. "The names may differ across Greek, Roman and Norse lore, but pay attention to the stories. The stories within the relationships hold keys."

Architecture. The incredible structures around the world that people can conceive, then work together to create and bring to life. With nature serving as an irreplaceable muse. "One of the strongest shapes in nature is the triangle. So, then, it's no coincidence that the pyramids are shaped as they are. And I'm not just referring to the ones found in Egypt. Be sure to look around; there's more to find."

Languages. Notably Latin. "The mother of our own language. Because words evolve as well, kid, but they all come from someplace. For example, let's examine the word 'education', shall we? Do you know what it means?"

"Umm. Sort of? But now I'm guessing it's doesn't have to do with sitting in a desk for hours and hours."

"Ha. Not exactly. The root of the word, the *source* of the word, means 'to bring about from within'. That is what an education truly is. So long as you look within, you can find an education anywhere you are."

"So, you don't like school? Me neither man, sitting around gets boring after a while."

"School is fine. And that's where you should be right now, hopefully with great teachers and classmates. But I look at school a little differently."

"Sideways? Upside-down, perhaps? Ha. Ha." Joe sniffles a mild laugh at Jimmy's commentary. "No. In my view, school never ends."

Jimmy's eyes blasting wide open, "WHAT?!? Please tell me that isn't so! Please?!?"

"Well, in my sideways and perhaps upside-down view, life is the teacher, and the world is the classroom. And the lessons she prepares for us never cease."

"Huh." Joe's philosophy finds a home in the young boy.

Joe also enjoys Jimmy's company whether sitting on the park

bench or walking through the winding paths of Collins Park. Sensing as though the boy is beginning to grasp the deeper meaning in their rolling conversation, the tie that binds. The bridge between Jimmy and Joe strengthening with each passing lesson. Underneath their bond, though, the raging waters and depths of the abyss with Slav grow more powerful as well.

Time continues to pass for all parties, life continuing to offer her lessons in several different forms in the years Jimmy grows from scrawny preadolescence into a taller version as a teenager. Not yet fully filling out his physique.

All the while, the dichotomy of Jimmy's life playing out in the days and nights spent in Collins Park and at Mom's house. Joe weaving a tapestry of wisdom while the sun shines high above. Imparting life's teachings with a steady and calming voice. Slav weaving a tapestry of fear as darkness descends upon the day. Imparting a different set of teachings with a similarly steady and yet insidious voice.

Oddly enough, though, Jimmy doesn't mention the interactions with Slav to his mentor during their time together. Just thinking the whole experience is something ordinary. That's what everyone lives with next door, isn't it?

If indeed life does prepare the lessons *for* us, then what might these lessons be for? And what could possibly narrow the space between the light and the darkness?

A Cadillac, A Brown Bag and Roy Orbison

11

SUMMER AGAIN. 1993. JIMMY A FEW YEARS OLDER AND PERHAPS EVEN A LITTLE BIT WISER. PERHAPS, AS ADOLESCENCE IS NOW IN FULL BLOOM. THE SEASON BRINGS MORE BLISTERING SUNSHINE DURING THE DAY ALONG WITH THE HAZY AND HUMID NIGHTS. WITH EACH PASSING YEAR, JIMMY GROWS MORE COMFORTABLE IN THE HEAT. HE WELCOMES IT, IN FACT.

The borders of the neighborhood expanding, too. One year of high school in the books now, so there are new horizons to explore. His favorite class as a freshman at the Jesuit prep school he attends? Latin. Jimmy now comfortably ventures past the sanctuary bound by Fifth Street. Riding his black Mongoose bicycle all around town, traveling to wherever the next game is, wherever his friends are. Whether it be backyards, ball fields or basketball courts.

His life moving a bit quicker, even in the dog days of summer. More friends, bigger experiences. Life opening up.

Yet, after all these years, nothing beats summer in Bayonne.

One Friday night, Jimmy finds himself home alone. A peaceful respite from a busy week around town. Staying home alone happens more and more these days. Mom is at a charity event and Bryan at a house party in Jersey City with his circle of friends.

The days of visiting the Little League every night fading by now. Jimmy growing older and perfectly content being home by himself. Happy watching the pros on TV, reenacting their every move in his living room. Picturing himself in the dugout getting ready for the sprint to take the field. Toeing the rubber on the pitcher's mound, feeling the energy of the crowd during his warm up tosses. His arm feels electric as he watches the teams take the field, geared up to paint a masterpiece tonight. The solitude allows him to create his own baseball paradise. One where anything is possible. Even using the TV announcers for his own play by play.

Plus, no one like Mr. Bexton around to disrupt the flow of the game.

Around nine o'clock that night, Jimmy hears a car pull up to the curb outside the house. Strange, as he certainly isn't expecting anyone. Bryan is supposed to be home much later tonight, if at all. Hopefully nothing happened to him. Walking across the living room, his beaten-up Rawlings still in hand, peering out Mom's ivory vertical blinds to see who it is. The visitor is not anything he recognizes from the neighborhood.

The car is a white Cadillac. Four doors each with opaque black tinted windows. Chrome rims on the wheels reflecting the amber street light above. A familiar bass thundering inside. What's that song? He knows it from somewhere.

Highly unlikely to be Bryan's ride home. But, wait a second. The passenger door opens, the lyrics of the song emanate full throttle. *That's* it. That's the song. "Insane in the Brain" by Cypress Hill. Bryan has been playing the new album on loop recently. Maybe it is Bryan's ride home?

Just then, a man steps out dressed in black jeans and an oversized white t-shirt, with light brown Timberland boots and a White Sox cap serving as the bookends for his ensemble. Jimmy notices he's holding a brown paper bag. It's not Bryan's ride home. Jimmy grows increasingly nervous. "Oh man. That guy coming *here*?" Panic starts to set in. "Damn. What do I do?" Quickly making sure the front door is locked. Check. Back door? Nah. Not yet. Lowering the lamp nearest the front window, now allowing him to peek through the vertical blinds undetected.

His pulse quickens. Beads of sweat beginning to trickle down his brow. Palms clammy. "Damn. What if he really is coming here?" Whatever you do don't answer the door. Head out the back. Hop the fences. Book it up to Casanova's house.

Good. Finally, a plan. An *escape* plan. Jimmy sits anxiously at the window as the man begins sauntering towards the house.

HUH? What's he doing? Instead of taking the stairs on the right towards Jimmy's house, the man instead swings left and walks up Slav's steps. Two loud knocks follow on Slav's door, the screen door creaks open, banging against the metal awning. A brief interaction follows, Jimmy unable to hear exactly what they say. It's not cordial, but it's not antagonistic either. After less than 30 seconds together, the man returns to the car. The white Cadillac with the shiny chrome rims drives away just as stealthily as it arrived. The sound of the bass in the speakers drifting off into the night.

"What was *that*? No one has ever come to see Slav. Ever."

About a half hour later, the quiet of the night and Jimmy's imaginary baseball game come to an abrupt halt. A radio screeches as it kicks on inside Slav's house, followed by BLARING music! The volume cranked to the maximum. Jimmy can feel the speakers pulsating behind the thin plaster wall. At this point, structurally weakened from years of pounding at Slav's behest. Then…

Singing…*singing*??

Slav is singing. "What in the *world* is going on?" Slav's typical Friday evening screaming session replaced with a slurring, sloshing cacophony of sounds. "Slav's turn to throw a party, I guess," Jimmy quips aloud to no one in particular.

The radio continues to play one song and one song only. An incessant loop. Maddening. Jimmy knows this song too. It's Roy Orbison's "Pretty Woman". The parents play it at parties, everyone always singing along. Especially the dad's, serenading the women after a few beers: "Pretty Woman…walkin' down the street….Pretty Woman…the kind I'd like to meet…". Jimmy knows the sounds of someone singing when they had a few.

A thought dawning on him just then. The brown bag? An instant later, it came to him. Oh man. The brown bag.

"Pretty Woman" ceaselessly playing over and over again. Slav's singing growing louder and louder with each woeful rendition. Maybe ten times in a row. Twenty? Jimmy easily losing count along the way. "My goodness, when is this guy going to stop? He has to go to bed soon, doesn't he? Just pass out already man, you already ruined my game."

Slav about to ruin a lot more than just his game.

BANG!! The wall starts to rattle. Again. And again. And again. Fist after fist angrily pounding the plaster barrier between the houses. "Heeere we go," Jimmy thinks to himself. Thunderous rage building along with each punch. Slav still singing during the rampage. BOOM. Pretty woman…BOOM… the kind I'd like to meet…BOOM. The violent force of each blow leaves Jimmy feeling as if the wall might crack wide open.

"I now you're home!! You little shit! I know you're theeer-ree." Slav directing his slurred ramblings towards the teenage boy next door. Jimmy sprints to the front door again to triple check the it's locked. Quickly racing to the back of the house as well, making sure the back door to the deck is secure. Just in case.

"I **HATE** you, kid! And I **HATE** your brother, too!"

"Yeah. Yeah. Heard it all before." Jimmy can easily picture the exact spot where Slav is standing as the onslaught continues. Back in his usual spot on the other side of the landing at the bottom of the stairs. Mentally picturing his wardrobe of the stained white shirt and light blue shorts. The club-like size of his fist. The image burning further into his mind with each strike against the wall.

"Great, here we go again," Jimmy mumbles out loud as he plops down into the recliner. His game ruined, his night ruined. Least he could do is finish watching the Braves on TV. That sounds like a minor victory.

This time, though, Slav's threats become uglier. Somehow nastier. Specific. No longer the broad sweeping threats he received in the past: "I know what room you sleep in kid! I'll be *right next door*. Waiting for you while you sleep! Knock. Knock. On the other side. I'll be right there as you try to dream. Only, I'll be your nightmare waiting!"

Oh God. He's right. Jimmy's room is the only bedroom in the house sharing a wall with Slav's. The thought of Slav being right on the other side of a wall, knocking while he sleeps, leaves him absolutely terrified. A growing pit in his stomach, goosebumps race up and down his arms.

"I'm not coming for your wussy brother anymore. Oh no, I want YOU, Jimmy boy! I want the little one now!! Young and fresh." Until this very moment, Jimmy didn't even realize Slav knew his name. "I'm going to make you my slave, boy. Teach you how to show respect, and you'll do whatever the hell I say! Any time mommy and your pathetic brother aren't there to protect you!"

Fist after fist slamming in sync with the menacing promise. "When they leave...you're mine."

Petrified. No one to call. Not going to call Mom home from her event, she deserves a fun night out. Plus, this would only upset her more. Bryan? No shot. He's partying, and it will take him too long to get home. I'll just tell him about it tomorrow.

But what to do now? Just keep the doors locked and stay quiet. Slav can't be serious. Can he? The rage and anger continuing— banging, singing, screaming— for another hour or so. Finally, mercilessly, the music stops. It's over.

But is it?

Thankfully, Slav doesn't attempt to kick the front door down. To claim Jimmy as his slave for the evening. Although Slav does accomplish his mission for the night, now raising the stakes in the game of living in fear of a monster next door.

Later that night, Jimmy walks carefully into his room, treading ever so lightly on his tippy-toes in order to avoid making any of the floorboards creak. Afraid to tip Slav off that it was his bedtime. As he opens the door, the moon casts its light through the small window and into his tiny sanctuary, illuminating the décor. The room can only fit a twin-sized bed, an undersized desk and a dresser. There isn't much space otherwise and given his growth spurt it's become easy for Jimmy to reach his dresser for clothes while still lying in bed. Regardless of the size, though, this is the one place in the whole house that's his. And his alone. He waited years for a room of his own, nagging Mom until she finally gave in, only when Bryan said he was too old for bunk beds and wanted his own space.

He gazes over to the wall he shares with Slav, the one his bed is pushed up against. What was once a blank space is now a masterwork he takes tremendous pride in. The entire wall is lined with sports posters, all fitting perfectly together from end to end, top to bottom. A seamless mosaic of his athletic heroes: Bo Jackson, Nolan Ryan, Mark McGwire, Will Clark, Michael Jordan. He patiently saved countless allowances to bring his vision to life. Now, he fears even being close to it.

Stealthily crawling under the covers, Jimmy waits in the darkness for the knocking to come. His only comfort is the raggedy black and brown stuffed puppy dog he cradles near his face. It was a present from the Easter Bunny year and years ago. As a little boy, he named the gift "Swoofy". Jimmy never wanted to let him go after that Easter. And he doesn't want to let him go tonight, either. The plush animal's fur dutifully absorbing his tears as he tries to fall asleep. A noble guard dog shielding him from what lays on the other side of the wall.

Jimmy barely sleeps a wink that night. Arising in the morning groggy and bit sour. Thankfully, no knocking came. He'll take that as a win. However, during breakfast, Jimmy decides against sharing what happened with Bryan. He's too tired from barely sleeping, and Bryan is also too tired from barely sleeping, albeit for an entirely different reason.

From that point forward, though, each weekend, the terrifying events of that night become standard. A new normal emerging. An evolution.

Mom and Bryan would leave for the night, each for a respective night out of fun and blowing off steam. Jimmy would stay home alone. Like clockwork, the white Cadillac with the shiny chrome rims appears under the streetlight. Transporting the delivery man with the brown bag. Then Roy Orbison and Pretty Woman.

Always accompanied by pounding against the wall. At times, Slav opens his front door, feigning an invasion of the home next door. Violent, callous threats to submit Jimmy to servitude.

On nights when he isn't too incapacitated, Slav follows through on his threat to torment Jimmy's sleep. The knocks and scratches on the wall begin just after midnight. The whispers in the darkness. "You will learn to respect me."

Jimmy learns to sleep in spells.

A month or so goes by, the exhausting new weekend sequence firmly established between Slav and Jimmy. Internally, he maintains his silence, not telling anyone in the family of the brown bags and verbal atrocities. He's not embarrassed or shy about it. Instead, viewing the episodes differently, as something natural. This is just the way it, the way it is *supposed* to be.

The family suspects life with Slav has tempered down, perhaps the period of storms has subsided. After all, he's is quiet now, laying possum for the nights when the boy is alone.

Something finally gives, though. A window into the new world Jimmy lives in. Broad daylight on a Saturday afternoon. Collins Park bustles with activity. A softball tournament is taking place a few hundred yards from the house at the field outside Salty's cart.

Jimmy looks on from the top step as the crowds gather. "Hope Salty's stocked up on dogs, buns and Marlboro reds. He's going to be busy today!" Smiling at the thought of Salty working up a sweat, smoking his trusty cigarettes, not saying a word to anyone, save for a crusty "dolla for the dawg". Mom opens the screen door, purse nestled under her arm. She's on her way over to the tournament to meet a few friends and watch their girls play.

"Have fun Mom."

"Come by later if you get bored. I'm sure everyone would like to see you."

"Okay, maybe later. Going to throw the ball around a bit first."

"Please do. I'm sure the other mom's would get a kick out of how much you've grown."

Jimmy's body is in the midst of an epic growth spurt. All in all, this summer he will grow nine inches. *Nine.* Rising from five-feet four inches at the end of the school year to six-feet one at the beginning of the next. The idea of Mom showing off his gangly body that now feels like spaghetti noodles for arms and legs isn't all that appealing.

"We'll see." Jimmy's red cheeks signaling his comfort level with the notion.

"I think it would be nice if you did. Anyway, your brother should be home soon. He went to get a haircut with Vito."

"Cool. Maybe we'll all head over then." Bryan and Vito are the perfect cover, easy for Jimmy to let them take the spotlight.

Jimmy grabs his tennis ball and glove, skipping down the steps to the driveway. He treats the driveway like bullpen in a major league stadium these days, having outgrown the distance leading to the front steps. The slope of the driveway is nearly identical to the mounds he pitches on, while the sturdy garage door operates as the backstop. A perfect way to practice taking grounders while getting some pitching in. Two birds with one stone.

Thwack. Thwack. Thwack. The ping of a tennis ball meeting the aluminum garage door. His arm is loosening up. With each throw Jimmy proceeds to increase velocity. The game beginning in his mind's eye.

He hears a car pulling down the block, radio blasting. He recognizes the beat, Run-DMC's "Down with the King" on full blast. The Cadillac? Now?

Beep. Beep. "Hey kid, get outta the friggin way!" Oh, that familiar accent. Barely audible over the sound of the speakers in Bryan's tiny black Toyota Camry. Vito.

The car pulls up and parks under the streetlight in front of the house. Same spot as the white Cadillac. Bryan slouching so low behind the wheel Jimmy can only see his fresh haircut.

They let the volume of the radio linger at the max level for a few moments after putting the car in park. "It's for effect," Bryan would later say. What kind of effect? Jimmy has no idea.

"Looks like Chopshop did a pretty good job on you boys. Let's check the neck though. Any blood? Little extra love from Charlie? No. Winner winner chicken dinner boys!" The three of them laugh together on the sidewalk. Vito walks up to Jimmy to give him a pound hug. "How's them burgers treating you, Jimmy boy?" He's referring to Jimmy's summer job as the short order cook at the Bayonne Community Pool. Working the flat top grill all morning and afternoon. Finally, a Saturday off.

"All good, man. I like it there." Thankfully the boys don't notice Jimmy blushing and nervously fiddling with the tennis ball. This summer, he met a girl there. A lifeguard named Quinn.

Bryan and Vito too wrapped up in their own plans. Feeling especially good heading into what the evening has in store for them. "All right bro, me and V gotta go get ready for tonight. Party over at Jackrabbit's. You chillin' here, or are you going over with Mom?"

"Going to hang here. Want to throw some more."

"Cool, bro. Have fun." Bryan and Vito turn to head up the stairs and into the house, looking for a quick turnaround before heading over to Jackrabbit's. They see who decided to join the pre-party.

Slav stands blocking the stairs to Mom's house. Bloodshot eyes and spit foaming in the corner of his mouth. His resemblance more akin to a rabid dog than a "friendly" neighbor next door. Jimmy spots that his right fist is clenched shut.

Damn. Now Jimmy wishes he told Bryan about the brown bags. About how Slav has been getting worse. Too late. Slav crossed the threshold. Breaching the demilitarized zone for the first time. All four of them stand still.

Each person eyeing the other side up as the standoff begins.
Vito knows some of the history, having experienced it at Bryan's
parties, yet is new to this kind of house party. Jimmy is anxious
about how he'll respond. Vito doesn't take any crap. Ever.

Vito, or simply V as his friends call him, is another 2nd Gen.
His grandparents emigrating from Sicily in the early 1900's. V's
father and uncle own and operate a demolition company. No
one really asks any other questions about the family business.
Everyone simply knows better.

V has smooth jet-black hair and a soft, silky voice. As if his
natural tone is slightly above a whisper. An uber talented goalie
on the high school soccer team, inking a Division One scholarship before his junior season. Jimmy has known him for as long
as he can remember. Truth be told, it's probably even longer.

The confrontation among the three, Slav, Bryan and Vito,
quickly grows more antagonistic by the minute. Jimmy fades
to the background, content with being a bystander for this one.
He's had his fill lately.

Escalating quickly to pushing, shoving, yelling. Each time
Slav claiming the role of victim, "Why won't you let me pass?"
yelling loudly as he stands his ground. "Let *us* pass, sir." Bryan
calmly requests. "That's my house, sir. We are just trying to go
inside." Bryan's immense patience on full display. Knowing
that cars parking across the street have probably already noticed
the disagreement.

Slav continually provoking the two boys. "Why are you speaking to me like that? Don't you have any respect for your elders?"

"Sir, we are asking you to move so we can go into the house."

Slav intent on causing a scene for everyone to witness. To
goad the boys into making the mistake of a lifetime. Pushing
the envelope, coveting a physical altercation. "I have half a
heart. Why are you picking on me? I'm just a poor man that

lives alone. I have health problems." His voice reverberates through the neighborhood.

Jimmy notices several neighbors peeking out their front windows. Witnessing the altercation through their lace curtains. Not one of them steps outside to intervene. With each passing comment, Slav drawing closer in front of the two boys, negating their desire to pass.

Finally, V hits his limit. "Bah fungoo!" waving his hand in Slav's face. Jimmy understands the polite English translation of the phrase means something like "stick it up your ass."

Vito continues on. A disgusted look on his. "Half a heart? You got no heart, you fat slob. You try to scare us, scare our little brother?" pointing to Jimmy in the driveway. Then pausing, walking within an inch of Slav's face: "Va fangul. You touch any one of us again, and they'll never find your body. Never. You understand me, Stunad?" Vito spits on the ground in front of Slav to seal the promise.

WHOOP WHOOP. Police sirens. The altercation now drawing the wrong kind of crowd. Two cruisers pulling up the driveway at Mom's house. "What's going on everyone?" the officer asking as she exits the passenger side of the first squad car. No answer from anyone. Slav finally quiet.

The two officers then separate the parties, beginning to take statements from each. Mom appears during the questioning, finally noticing what all the commotion was about. And looking none too pleased to see police cars outside of her house. The boys explain what happened. How Slav was blocking their way to the house. How he seemed to be looking for a fight. A real fight.

"Has he ever done anything like this before? Has he ever done anything to threaten you?" The officer's concerned look says it all.

"Well, yeah. He does." Bryan offers a simple answer.

"When was the last time he did?"

"Not for a while now. I don't even know to be honest."

"Uh. I do." Jimmy sheepishly enters the conversation from the backstage. Mom, Bryan, V and the officer all turn with looks of surprise on their faces. "Please, kid. Tell us what's been going on." Jimmy tells them about his recent experience. The deliveries of brown bags, the singing, the threats. He relays all of it, except what happens at night while he's trying to sleep. He doesn't need to. Concerned that someone might find out and make fun of him, say that Slav tries to sleep with him like the other creepers.

He's also lucky to finally have a room to himself and he wants to keep it that way.

Mom covers her mouth. Flummoxed with no idea what to say. Bryan and Vito are enraged. As if they could rip Slav's arms off and beat him with them this very moment. Maybe Vito's promise might come to fruition after all.

The officer calmly finishes taking the report. Upset at the contents; however, she knows how important the truth is. How vital this information is to whatever may come from here. She recommends speaking to a lawyer and seeking a restraining order against Slav. Imploring the family to have his behavior on record, because, well, you never know. "Especially if his behavior is beginning to escalate. That could lead to bad things."

As the officer returns to the squad car, she pulls Jimmy aside, "Kid, I'm glad you told us what's been happening with your neighbor. I know it wasn't easy, but that took a lot of courage. So just know you're one hell of a brave kid. I have your back. We all do."

Following the counsel and rationale from the officer, Mom went to court to obtain a restraining order against Slav a few weeks after the incident at the house. It doesn't have the intended effect.

The Third Law of Motion on display in the townhouses on First Street: for every action, there is an equal and opposite reaction.

Involving the courts only incenses Slav further. A restraining order against someone you share a wall with? Good luck with that. Like the officer mentioned, at least it's on record now. In case something happens. Or *when.*

The weeks roll along, and Slav expands his verbal onslaught unfazed. Daring the family to call the police and enforce the restraining order. He now willingly ventures outside. Sitting on his steps, berating the family as they walk into and out of their home.

Mom begins to use only the garage to come and go. Fearful for her life. Bryan snaps back each time. The white wrought iron railing again operating as a dividing line, at times the only space separating them from an all-out brawl. Jimmy keeps his head down. Avoiding eye contact. Racing in and out of his home every time, regardless of whether or not Slav is physically present.

When he is there, Slav greets Jimmy with an evil smile. And a message: "You're going to be mine, kid."

Summer nears a close. The dark clouds of a gathering storm. Slav's anger and hostility a near constant presence in the family's lives. Intensifying. To what end? This *has* to end, doesn't it?

Someone might know.

Another Harvest

_____

12

Jimmy hits the bend on the path behind the Pony League field, making straight aim for the fir tree near the water. He's on a quest for his friend. And sure enough, he finds who he is looking for right where he usually does. Seated on that park bench at the water's edge. Face down tracking his finger over the words of his book, same as always.

"Well, well, well. If it isn't Ferdinand Magellan himself?" Jimmy loudly jokes as he approaches his friend. "Or maybe Billy Shakespeare?" Up to the task, Carpenter Joe replies without even glancing up from his book. "To unpathed waters, undreamed shores." A welcoming smile across his face. "Boldness be my friend."

Jimmy returns the smile. Knowing he came to the right place. "Can I talk to you about something?" This time sure of the answer.

"Of course. Grab a seat."

Jimmy takes his customary seat on the bench, to the right-hand side of his mentor. Wasting little time getting to the crux of the matter. "You know who Slav is? My neighbor?"

"I do. Yes."

"Well, here's the thing…" Jimmy quickly launches a whirlwind of details. A barrage of commentary and colorful language. Eager to tell the tale. To *finally* tell the full story behind the nightmare next door. Hastily recounting the entire oral history of his, and his family's, nightmare with Slav. Years in the making now. How it started after the party Bryan threw way back when. "You remember that? It was a while ago, but it was his first one."

"I do recall that."

"Mom took care of it that night. But Slav kept going after that."

How it was no big deal at first. Just some crazy talk from a guy who was probably crazy. "Bryan and I would just laugh about it while we cleaned up. How Slav would threaten to beat us like dogs, kneel in a kitty litter box, stuff like that. We didn't take it too seriously."

"Is that so?" Joe's only response to Slav's vicious commentary. "Yeah. A lot of that and a lot about respecting him."

How long it's been happening. "Years now, Joe. Has to be something like four years now. I just never thought to mention it to you before."

"Kid, you can talk to me about anything, I know you know that. So why now? How can I help?"

"Well, things got real about a month or so ago." Jimmy informs Joe of how everything changed. When everything changed. "This white Cadillac with rims pulled up one night. A guy got out with a brown paper bag and delivered it to Slav's house. After that? Oh man. It started with him singing at first, you know that song "Pretty Woman"? Dear God…the guy plays it over and over again. Screaming to the words the whole time. I used to like that song, but I can't think of anything but Slav when I hear it now."

Slav's behavior escalating. The knocking on Jimmy's bedroom wall in the middle of the night. "Wakes me up almost every night telling me I'm going to be his. At least it feels that way. Maybe it's the just the weekends. I honestly can't tell anymore. Keeps whispering I'm going to be his little slave, lock me up and teach me to show respect. Always ends with 'you're going to be mine, kid'." Jimmy mimicking Slav's unmistakable gruff voice.

"Things almost came to blows with Bryan and V, but the cops pulled up first. I told them a little about what was happening. They said that was a good thing. Me? I'm not so sure. Because they also said to get a restraining order against Slav."

Then the restraining order came and so did the blowback. "Slav sits outside now. Keeps trying to push us to go over the railing. Like he *wants* us to fight him or something. My friends won't even come over anymore because he scares the crap out of them. It's almost every day and every night now, Joe. Mom started using the garage only. Me and Bryan won't back down though. I take the steps quick, try not to listen to him if he's there."

Joe listens intently. Gripped by the story. Concern embedded in every facial feature: eyes squinted, lips pursed, head gently nodding "no". The cover of his book long closed, gently resting on his lap.

Finally, Jimmy finishes speaking. Taking a deep breath following the conclusion of his tale. Unfortunately, this story doesn't have an ending. At least not yet.

The two friends sit for a moment in silence. Joe considers the state of affairs and how best to help the boy and his family. Finally, the mentor speaks softly. "I'm sorry that you and your family are going through this. And while it may sound like an odd question, it's an important one: do you think this will last forever?"

A surprisingly quick reply. "Nah. Something's gotta give, right? I just don't want it to be the bad way of giving, if you know what I mean?"

"I do. And I agree. Kid, clearly Slav is not well."

"Clearly, yeah, I picked up on that." Replying with a chuckle. Witnessing enough of both Slav and people around town that weren't "well" to know Slav fits the mold. Only issue is that the other people didn't live next door and scare the hell out of him while he tries to sleep at night.

"Are you afraid of him, though?" Joe asked, keenly interested in the answer.

"Like, do I really think he is going to hurt me kind of afraid? I don't really think about it, not like that, anyway. But no. I'm not." It isn't the hardened "I'm not". Neither defiant nor stubborn, as Jimmy initially was about Mr. Bexton or Jimmy's dad. It is softer, yet clear and resolute. How about that? The boy isn't afraid. Despite the years of pounding against the walls of his home, the verbal threats, midnight whispers, the restraining order.

Joe isn't surprised by the answer, though. "And why is that?" he wonders aloud. "I don't know, really. I want to play ball and see where life goes from here. Like you said, this can't last forever. I just don't think it helps thinking about all the bad things that can happen. All the nasty stuff he says."

"I didn't say it wouldn't last forever. You did."

"Huh, I guess I did." A gentle smile accompanies the comment. "I just want to look at the orchard, Joe. Not some big tree in my way."

"Good to hear, kid. So then, aside from the tree removing itself, it appears you've discovered another way to see the orchard."

"I have?"

"You remember our apple tree conversation then, since you're focusing on the orchard, correct?"

"Yup, think about it a lot these days."

"Well, what's inside the apple?"

"Seeds." Confident in the answer, Jimmy congratulates himself.

"Good. Where are they?"

"Inside?" Jimmy wonders if a trick question has come into play.

"Good again. But where inside?"

"Uh…the middle?"

"In the core. The heart of the apple. The seeds you hold in *your* core, your *heart*, are the thoughts that help you see the world you wish to see. Be it the wide-open orchard or the singular tree." Jimmy laughs again. So simple, yet he never thought about the seeds that way. Never even considering the seeds before. Only that if you move the tree, then it's easier to see the orchard. Joe smiles inwardly, recognizing the lesson has found a place for Jimmy. Perhaps it's the first harvest of the orchard. He completes the understanding of seeds for the pupil. "What you *do* is a choice, and so is what you *see*."

The mentor transitions to another segment of Jimmy's relationship with Slav. New territory for them both. Treading lightly, but venturing forward nonetheless: "So, how do you *feel* towards Slav?"

Jimmy slightly taken back by the question. "*Feel?*" Feelings are meant to be felt, not talked about. "Do you mean if I hate him or anything like that?"

"If that's how you would like to put it, sure."

"No worries, I got you. Don't feel much of anything really. I'm prepared in case he does something, carry a little pipe with me like a set of brass knuckles, but I don't actually hate the guy or anything. He said one time he has half a heart. Who knows, maybe he does? I don't know if that's possible, but with him? Sure as heck might be." Jimmy pauses before continuing. Talking about feelings evidently comes naturally with his friend Joe. "Although, if he does something to me or my family, I might change my mind about that." Jimmy grins and raises his eyebrows for added emphasis.

"I understand. No judgement here." Joe assures him.

"Why all the questions about feelings and stuff? I mean, it is what it is. Just stuff I have to deal with."

"First, feelings matter. Know that. Second, well, second can wait. I have one more question before that."

An eye roll from the boy, "Here we go again." But Jimmy is fully invested now, and he came asking for help, so there's no way of squirming out of the inquisition. Reluctantly nodding for Joe to proceed with the verbal examination.

"How are you so *sure* Slav won't do something bad to you or your family?"

Jimmy's face twists as he ponders the question, partially to figure out what Joe is driving at. A moment or two passing: "I'm not sure. I just wanna think about other things instead. High school. Playing ball for a long time. Meeting people, maybe even a girl? Traveling. I'd like to see some of those places you talk about. You know, the ones with the beautiful views. The amazing people. Who knows?"

Jimmy glances over to his mentor, meeting him eye to eye. The wonder of his youthful teenage face providing a window into his soul. He continues his train of thought. "I'd sure rather think about that than being locked away inside Slav's house."

A lifetime of wisdom wrapped in the modest statement of a teenager.

"I don't think I need to make the second point. You just took care of that one for me." A quizzed look appears on Jimmy's face. He is still expecting clarity on the second point. "Okay then, my second point was about something called certainty." Jimmy's befuddled look shifts, his spine straightens, somatically acknowledging he is familiar with the concept. "I know the word. Don't know what it has to do with Slav, though."

Joe considers the point. "What if I said the only thing certain about Slav is that you aren't certain what he is going to do. He is, let's say, certainly uncertain. How's that sound?"

"I get it. Sounds real to me."

"Life is full of uncertainty. That's why *IF* is the very heart of the word." Cementing the lesson, Carpenter Joe continues. "The search for certainty is often rooted in fear. Take Slav, one way to be *certain* he does not harm you would be to stay inside your house at all times. Yet here you are, going about your life in the midst of this uncertainty. Acknowledging the fear, but not choosing that path. Instead, focusing on where you want to go, the orchard, if you will. The boundless possibilities of the paths in front of you, of *how* you wish to live *your* life. All that is required after that is action."

"I'm more afraid of *not* doing what I want to, Joe. Or of Slav winning."

"It would be wise not to let fear of any kind spur your action. So, focus your intentions on what you *do* want. Just know that when you're the captain of the ship, you get to decide who comes on board. I have a feeling you are meant for deep waters, and it doesn't sound like Slav is a welcomed shipmate as of now."

"Ha. I think our quarters are close enough as they are now. But what if it gets worse? What if Slav does do something?" Joe shoots back without hesitation, "What if it gets better? What if what Slav decides to pack up and leave town? Remember living with 'if' is why we call it *life*. It's your choice how you want to look at the 'if'."

"I get it, Joe." As he sits considering the 'what ifs', Jimmy begins to smile, then laughing to himself. Joe sees Jimmy's lighthearted reaction and begins to laugh gently himself. "What are you laughing at, you silly goose?"

Jimmy offers insight to the joke. "Just reminds me of something Cas says all the time, one of those common sayings that isn't true."

"And what's that?"

"If my grandmother had balls, she would have been my grandfather." Jimmy laughs louder and shakes his head as he shares Casanova's wisdom. Joe greets him with a smile in return. "Not sure that one is all that common. The truth, though?"

"Truth is, my grandmother has way bigger balls than a lot of guys I've come across." Jimmy belly laughs as the words come out. "Like you said, just depends on how you look at the 'if'." He then respectfully nods to his mentor. One harvest reaped. Another planted.

"Now *that's* perspective." Joe laughs at the simple genius of it. "And that's something to carry with you. Just remember kid, Slav can't harm what's inside *here*." Joe points his calloused right index finger at Jimmy's heart. A wink of his left eye accompanying the final teaching for the day.

The Certainty of Uncertainty

13

JIMMY AND JOE CONTINUE ON THE BLACK ASPHALT PATH, ROUNDING PAST THE DOG PARK ON THEIR RIGHT-HAND SIDE. IN THE PRESENT MOMENT, A GORGEOUS AUTUMN DAY UNFOLDS AROUND THEM.

Now drawing closer to the back side of the Little League field. The massive steel arches of the Bayonne Bridge rounding into view. A few more people fill the playground to near capacity now. Parents and their children. Jimmy quickly noticing the ages of the kids are nearly identical to his own. The vision of his sons and daughters immediately bursts to mind. Is there anything better than seeing their imagination at play? Pretending to be treasure hunters on a great ocean adventure as they climb a fiberglass pirate ship?

The noontime sun is high in the sky, giving greater ease to the late Fall chill in the air. Although the conversation isn't necessarily following the same thawing process. Sunlight may expose the truth, but it can also cast very long shadows, too.

"I know where you're going with this, Joe. And I do appreciate it. I get it, really, I do." Jimmy's frustrations with the reflections of his life only beginning to float away.

"And what exactly is it that you get?" Joe feigning a look of surprise.

"Uncertainty. Life is uncertain. Be prepared for anything but make your choice for how you want to live your life."

Joe stops, turning towards Jimmy, and starts clapping. A gentle golf clap. "Well, look at you, always learning something. Especially something you've learned years ago as a boy. Knocked that one out of the park, kid." Sarcasm dripping from every syllable. Jimmy gives Joe a crooked look, slightly annoyed at the gesture. But realizing quickly enough it isn't mean spirited.

Don't take it personal.

Also knowing well enough by now that it means there is more to learn. Following the standing ovation, Joe continues walking, drawing closer to the Little League field. "So, what does all of this mean for you *now*?" Joe inquires.

Jimmy provides a swift response. "Move forward. Be who I'm meant to be." Intending to head Joe off at the pass.

"And have you figured out who that is yet?"

Silence. Jimmy slows the pace of his walk, a wistful comment following a moment or two, "Well, I'm starting to. Or, at least I think I'm starting to."

"I see. Admitting you're a little lost is a noble first step. After all, being lost is different than being stuck."

"Tell me something, though Joe, why Slav? There are plenty of other people or experiences in my life that explain uncertainty."

Jimmy rattles them off one by one. As if back in the board room presenting a corporate slide deck.

His father. "Whether he was ever coming back? Whether he even knew who I was?" Coaches. "Some good. Some bad. Some great. Some that were bad then became great." College. "Picking a school. Hoping it was the right one. Even what came after that, since…"

Jimmy pauses ever so briefly before resuming his monologue. Blinking his eyes, returning again to the present moment.

Relationships. "Long distance with Quinn. Then whether we could have a family together." Corporate America. "Year after year told I was a respected leader, someone that carries the business forward, then in the same breath, being told I was replaceable. That management's perception is reality, and I need to adjust to their view, to respect their judgement as absolute." Jimmy finally concludes the oral presentation. "Whoever and wherever, Joe. There isn't a part of my life where it wasn't present."

Joe offers a stoic response. "True. All valid examples, but they merely point out that we are in agreement."

"About what?"

"That the only thing certain about life is uncertainty," Joe affirms with undeniable candor. Jimmy's head tilts sideways, brows furled. Thinking about the comment momentarily. "Yeah, Joe. We agree on that. Still."

"Good then. *Knowing* that life is uncertain is quite important, because we can then discuss the shadow side of uncertainty."

"What in the world does *that* mean?"

"When we choose to see the uncertainty, there is a shadow behind it that we merely care to glimpse at from time to time. Unwilling to shine the light any further to expose the truth." Jimmy is confused, "I don't get it. What does that have to do with uncertainty? Light and shadows. Wouldn't uncertainty just *be* the shadow?"

Joe expands on the wisdom found in the darkness. "Until we see all things in light, there will be shadows. And what lies in the shadow of uncertainty produces a powerful reaction. One that holds us back from experiencing all that we are meant to."

"And what's that?"

"Judgement. We judge what we cannot see in the uncertain shadows. The places we are unwilling to step into, the people we are unwilling to speak with. All that we are unwilling to cast a light on, and at times unwilling to *be* the light. Instead, we rest in the comfort of life being uncertain, content with our narrow view of the shadows from afar."

"Whoa, hold up a second. Joe, who am I passing judgement on? Who am I to even be able to pass judgement?"

"We all do. It is part of humanity, a shadow cast by all of her beauty. A conditioned response to the human condition."

"Well what in the world do I have to do to change that?"

"Hmm. You asked me why Slav, correct?"

"Sure did."

"Do you remember how it ended?" Joe raises his eyebrows and the intonation of his voice as he asks the question. Immediately Jimmy's face lights up, eyes growing wide. "Oh, wow. How could I ever forget *that*?" Jimmy audibly blowing air from his mouth as he answered. "That was *wild*." The flood of memories rushing back in vivid color. Years since he thought about the ending. *YEARS*. Jimmy's eyes let go of the memory and fade back into the current moment, "But what does that have to do with anything?"

Joe grins. Another harvest to reap.

"Because uncertainty isn't the only lesson Slav taught you."

SECTION FOUR

Cracking the Coconut

An Irish Luau

14

JIMMY NAVIGATES THE SWELTERING SUMMER
NIGHTS IN THE CITY WITH EASE BY 1997. A COUPLE
OF DECADES OF EXPERIENCE UNDER HIS BELT IN THE
BAYONNE HEAT TO THANK FOR THAT.

Wearing the constant glisten of sweat and the red tinged
sunburn on the back of his neck as a badge of honor from his
day job working as a landscaper. The only downside to the
landscaping job is that it takes him away from the ballfields all
day. Each of the boys with summer jobs now, though. It's been
that way since high school.

Jimmy chose to move on from his stint as a short order cook.
An easy decision once Quinn made the move to work down the
shore all summer long. Lifeguarding at the pool replaced by
a breakfast gig at a mom and pop pancake house. That frees
up her afternoons for the beach. She visits the city from time
to time but prefers her sandy-toed lifestyle to the static air and
closed toe shoes of Bayonne.

For Jimmy, this summertime profession is the best outcome
he could conceive of. After all, he's still able to play in the

grass and dirt all day long. Actually being paid for it is a bonus in his view.

The air is still thick from the humidity, but also thick with something else these days. Opportunity. The college years are here for Jimmy. The big wonderous world continues to open up grander every single day. New friends, new experiences, new possibilities. But before the chapters containing those dreams can be written, one chapter in his life must come to a close.

In the years following the conversation between Jimmy and Joe about the certainly uncertain Slav, the new normal of life with his neighbor rolled forward unabated. *More* visits from the white Cadillac. *More* brown bags delivered to Slav's front door. *More* Roy Orbison. *More* "Pretty Woman". The regiment continuing on: *More* violent threats to the boys. Murder. Arson. Castration. All commonplace by now.

However, something else took place as Slav's days grew darker. Bryan and Jimmy grew too. Taller. Stronger. More confident. Bryan filling out his powerful, broad frame, now spending his final summer at home before beginning a job as a "Big Five" accountant in New York. He is scheduled to move to Hoboken come September. One more summer of fun for him before "the real world" sets in.

Jimmy himself blossoming into a full six-foot three and 185 pounds. Square shouldered, lean and powerful. Every bit the athletic frame he once envisioned. The bespectacled string bean of yesteryear long gone by now.

The "little" brother has now become the "younger" brother.

Jimmy still doesn't fear Slav mentally, hasn't for years, but now his physical strength matches his mental fortitude. For starters, he no longer sprints up the steps to avoid Slav. Instead, Jimmy walks. Slowly. Even if Slav sits on his stoop muttering profanities or stands lurking in his doorway shadows, Jimmy continues to walk. Meeting Slav's menacing stare eye to eye. Still hearing the same sadistic ramblings as always, only now each word uttered from Slav bounces off his muscular shoulders.

Dust to brush off.

Finally, after years of running or sneaking into his own house, Jimmy takes back his own front stairs. The simple task of walking into his house wholly unafraid leaves him with an impossibly good feeling. Oh yes, the stairs are his again. What can he conquer next?

Jimmy still plays summer league ball this year. Latching on to a couple of local teams, always searching for reps and an opportunity to play. "Hopefully a couple more summers in the sun," he says to himself while packing his gear.

A few injuries playing college ball hamper him now, so he's not quite sure what the future of the sport is for him. His back and right shoulder giving way to herniated discs and nerve damage. No matter, though. He keeps playing hard and enjoying every minute of it. Giving it everything he has. No regrets.

One other wonderous opportunity arrives during this season of life. A rite of passage now nearing completion. It's Jimmy's turn to host parties at Mom's house. Having learned from one of the best in Bryan, Jimmy is now eager to put his own unique twist on the on this time-honored family tradition.

Interestingly enough, Jimmy doesn't drink alcohol. He explored it once in high school and didn't like who he became under the influence. Or the headache the next day. Memories of his father becoming too real for him. The apple tree taking root back in the orchard. One night and that was it. Confident enough to take a stand, even if the boys didn't quite understand it. Jimmy swore not to drink again until he knew he could handle what comes with it. The boys respected his decision without reservations, strengthening the bonds of friendship.

This apple wants to make sure the tree doesn't have a second run in the orchard.

Being sober isn't going to deter him from being a bourgeoning superstar party planner though. Quite the contrary, actually. Jimmy prides himself on creating epic nights of "legendary fun" for all. Drinking isn't the point of the party; bringing everyone, and he means *everyone*, together is.

The summer of '97 holds his best idea yet. A golden ticket to cement his legacy. And perhaps take the mantle of best in the business from Bryan once and for all.

The thought hits him like a rogue wave while digging a ditch one afternoon. What if we hosted a midsummer classic? "Heck, if the major leagues do it every summer, why can't we? We'll just change it up a little." Or, rather, change it up a lot. The theme for this stroke of genius? An Irish Luau. The magnificent details all simultaneously rushing into his consciousness.

Jimmy sprints into the house following his day in the dirt, bouncing upstairs in three leaps while making a beeline to his room. Time to let the boys know. We need to rally the squad. Whistling as he picks the phone next to his bed to call Casanova. Fingers dancing as they speed through the digits.

"Cas, what's up brother. Check this out, our Moms are heading down to AC in a couple weeks for an overnight to hit the slots and stuff. I got an idea. Can you loop in Sweetness and Jaws? I'll see if Broomstick and Picasso are around."

"That's awesome, man. Yeah, I'll hit the three-way now. Hold on."

A double three-way call. The ultimate party planning mastermind. A few moments later, Casanova clicks back with Sweetness and Jaws. Jimmy secures a line with Broomstick and Picasso, a new member to the crew, joining during high school.

Jimmy ticks through the plan and execution like it's straight out of *Mission: Impossible.* "Boys, listen up, I got something for you. An Irish Luau. Two weeks from now. Mom's house."

"What the frig is that?" Casanova ever so politely interjecting.

"Let me explain, please, before you get all jumpy like your brother. We set an island scene, have tasty drinks, and dress the part. Think plenty of booze plus a whole lot of tiki."

"Okay, I'm intrigued. Please continue." Cas graciously allows Jimmy to resume the discussion. "Thank you. I will. And since you chimed in first, Cas, you're on decorations. Plus, since the Moms are going together, I *know* you have nothing else going on that day. We are going to need tiki torches, lots of them."

"Fine. Fine. I'll set the mood." Casanova's mind drifts immediately to a scantily clad paradise.

"Good. Broom, bartender, so you got drinks. We need two kegs and a kickass Hawaiian Punch. I have some recipes."

"Done." Broomstick doesn't leave a lot of meat on the bone when he speaks, either.

"Nice. Thanks. Picasso, DJ for the night. You know what to do."

"Surest I do. We will dance and sing in merriment." Picasso, an artsy fellow, owns a CD library that would make a radio station envious. Plus, he has a six CD spinner so the music can keep rolling all night long.

"Perfect man for the job, thanks. Jaws. Do what you do best brother: spread the word." When word of mouth is the fastest form of communication, its best to have the fastest mouth broadcasting it.

"I just told fifty people...in my mind...HAHA!!" Classic Jaws. The only thing faster than his mouth is his wit.

Jimmy still laughs as he continues. Beaming as the execution plan unfolds brilliantly. "Sweetness, social chair. Let's make sure we don't have all that weird awkwardness when people first arrive. We want them to feel at ease. Quickly."

"Yeah, one problem though, pal."

"What's that?"

"Who, pal. Slav. What do we do about him? He only gives us till 10 then he calls the cops." Sweetness, a future politician, or litigator, or both. Flawlessly adept at bringing any conversation back down a few notches of reality.

Jimmy purses his lips. A quick pivot springs to mind. "Eh, he's been quiet lately. Hasn't threatened to kill me in like a week. It's a good point, though. Then let's start earlier. Mom's leaving around three o'clock that day to beat traffic. We start around five-thirty or six, offer dinner to everybody. I'll do burgers and dogs. Put the years at the pool to good use. How's that?"

"Perfect. Social chair it is. This is going to be fantastic."

"Thanks, boys. Knew you would like this idea. One more thing, though."

"What now?" Jaws chimes in. "I already told a hundred more people."

"I'm going to the store tomorrow to get grass skirts and coconut bras for us. And a few extras that we can hand out to guests to be part of the evening as well. How do you like that?" Casanova snaps back from his imaginary island utopia to rejoin the conversation. "Dude, you couldn't have just led off with that? Come on man, you mean to tell me I could possibly 'decorate' a certain set of our lovely patrons with grass skirts and coconut bras? This could have been a much quicker conversation."

"Save the best for last, right brother? Time to go big or go home. Or just go big *at* home. It's go time." Click. Click. Several more after that. The call ends. Execution begins.

The early start time certainly gives the party enough time to ramp into the fun, but Jimmy is mildly disappointed as he hangs up the phone. Damn Slav. Like a human rain cloud. Regardless, the Irish Luau is on. Too great of an idea to pass up.

Jaws spends the next two weeks lining up the guest list. Spreading the good word far and wide across New Jersey. No doubt, this is *definitely* a go.

Luau night finally arrives. The execution committee all weaving together seamlessly in their various roles and tasks. A well-oiled machine. Thankfully, Mother Nature cooperates wonderfully as well. Clear skies, the humidity easing, and the tiki torches providing the perfect ambiance while dutifully serving the dual purpose of keeping the mosquitoes at bay.

Friends coming from all over: Jersey City, Hoboken, Secaucus, Rutherford. Friends of friends and even other friends of theirs joining. Everyone dresses the part. Hula shirts everywhere, the girls with Hibiscus flowers in their hair, some folks even in bathing suits. Full regalia all around Mom's house. The crowd is definitely feeling it. Casanova on point with the decorations— of both people and place. Fellow expert Broomstick came through big time. The punch is a hit. And the punch also hits back, the recipe of wonders.

Mom's house and backyard at full capacity. Over a hundred people shoulder to shoulder from the front door to the back fence. Jaws spread the word. No doubt.

Outside, the top deck serves as the beating heart of festivities. The spot offers a perfect view of the lower deck and the various drinking games Sweetness prepared combined with a straight view of the dance hall inside the house. Picasso's DJ station sitting right on the dining room table just inside the sliding glass doors. The soundtrack he composed as eclectic as Bayonne itself, one song after another bringing a whole new level of excitement to the crowd: Pearl Jam "Even Flow". Wu

Tang Clan "C.R.E.A.M". The Doors "Break on Through". The Notorious B.I.G. "Hypnotize". U2 "I Still Haven't Found What I'm Looking For". A Tribe Called Quest "Award Tour."

Picasso's genius on full display with each track. And with every new song, the crowd's cheers grow louder, people dancing and singing along with the lyrics. New friends, old friends and everyone in between. All together. Everyone smiling.

It's magical to witness.

To Jimmy, though, one smile stands out in particular. Quinn's. She drove up from the shore for this. Even brought a few beach friends to introduce them to the crew. Their friendship from a few summers back working at the Bayonne Community Pool continues to grow. Funny how it all started when they look back now: Jimmy tipping his sweat-stained baseball cap to Quinn and a friend during a lunch break one afternoon. As a gentleman should to a lady. Quinn returning the gesture with her fabled smile.

From humble beginnings comes the start of a great adventure.

No way the absolutely beautiful blue-eyed girl from uptown would miss this. An Irish Luau? She has to experience this firsthand. "HI!" Quinn's smile, magnified by her golden tan, lights up as she walks into the tight kitchen quarters and lands a gentle kiss on Jimmy's cheek. A pink and purple Hibiscus lei highlight her festive ensemble. A matching purple flower in her hair.

"Oh, hey." Jimmy blushes immediately. "Thanks for coming up. You didn't have too." This is the first moment Jimmy ever wishes he had a drink in his hand. Not for the alcohol, but so he could hold something in in hands to stop them from fidgeting spastically while he clumsily attempts to make small talk. He's praying Quinn doesn't notice.

"Are you kidding? This is amazing. What a great idea! I brought my cousin and a few friends. Hope you don't mind, they really wanted to be here, too." Too? Jimmy catches the word and holds on tight. Quinn really wanted to be here. "Awesome. Have a blast. Just please tell your crew to be careful with the punch. Broom mixed up a heavy hitter."

"Oh, yikes. I will. Although I think my cousin had two glasses already." A pensive look replaces Quinn's joyous smile.

"No worries. I'll give her some water and will let Broom know to go light with the ladle."

"Thanks! This is going to be such an incredible night! My whole family would love this. I'll have to keep this idea in mind." Quinn's "whole" family is quite a large family tree, and large might be an understatement. There are twenty-four first cousins just on her mother's side.

"That's cool. Have a great time, and let me know if you need anything." Jimmy walks away towards the back deck, his hands mercifully stop gyrating and sweating. He peeks back for another look at the party's most important guest. In the middle of a raucous crowd of grass skirts, coconut bras and teenage lunacy, Jimmy is fixated on Quinn's stunning smile.

In Jimmy's eyes, her smile personifies *joy*.

For now, their friendship is just a friendship. Would it grow beyond that? That's not important tonight. She's here, and she really wanted to be here. Turns out seeds within a friendship grow too.

After sunset the party takes on a life of its own. Aloha spirit flowing freely on the Golden Peninsula. For Jimmy, seeing an idea come to life is one thing, but experiencing it surpassing all expectations is beyond compare. Who knew it could be this good?

A comfortable feeling settles in tonight. Jimmy enjoys being be around so much happiness. Everywhere he looks, each person relishing the night to the fullest. Laughing, singing, dancing. Much different than most nights he's endured the past few years.

Later in the night, out on the top deck, Sweetness and Jimmy stand together absorbing the moment. Bruce Springsteen's "Jersey Girl" playing full blast inside. Picasso now taking requests from the crowd. The largest karaoke session in Bayonne history currently underway.

Sweetness turns towards Jimmy: "Hey pal. This is A-mazing. I'm loving this. What time do you want people out of here though? Seems like it's starting to get a little late for the friendly neighbor next door."

"Whatever works. Mom is away until tomorrow, remember? Let's keep going and see what time Slav calls the cops on us. Just break it up after that. That work?"

"Sure. Works for me. I'm not looking to go anywhere, and I don't think anyone else is either! You better be enjoying yourself, bud. You earned it tonight!"

"I'm good, man. Just soaking it all in. What time is it anyway?" Jimmy asks, hoping for the earlier side. "A bit after 11. Like, almost midnight. Ha. Why?"

"Huh. Interesting. Please let everyone know they can stay if they need to. No driving. You know what I mean?"

"I gotcha. And I'm one of them! I'm calling couch right now! Casanova can hug the floor. He'll think he's curled up in an angel's lap no matter what. Holy frickin' Hawaiian punch!"

The party continues on until the early morning hours. The few stragglers without a safe ride home land in various spots throughout Mom's house. The morning scene resembling a fraternity house following Homecoming. In the end, the boys achieved an Irish Luau for the ages. Setting a new standard for house parties. Bryan's torch has officially been handed down. Along with a few mops for cleanup.

Remarkably, the police never show.

"Of all things I'm happy about from the luau, I'm especially glad that psycho next door didn't rat us out. Would have been a shame if he was home last night." Sweetness opens up the dialogue at the 8th Street Diner after a few hours of sleep.

"It's weird, though. I'm trying to figure that out. Maybe Slav was too drugged up from the beginning and just passed out," Jimmy reasons as their order of egg sandwiches and hash browns arrive.

"First time he hasn't called the cops, right? And we had a lot of people last night. A LOT. Ah, you're probably right, though. That has to be it." Sweetness washes down the greasy hash browns with a sip of black coffee.

Yup. That has to be it.

Finnegan's Block Party

15

The night following the luau, Jimmy has a baseball game in Jersey City. One more summer in the sun. In his heart, though, Jimmy knows this summer is likely his last.

Bryan offers to drive him. It's nice night to catch a game. Plus, he wants to hear *everything* about this Irish Luau and what made it so damn special that he's already fielded nine calls asking for him to host his own.

Even more impressive than the party itself is that when Mom arrived back at the house, the place was immaculate. "You have to tell me how you pulled this off, bro. Sounds like an awesome night. And Mom isn't even pissed about it either!" Bryan proclaims as they climb into the car. "Ha. I'll tell you about the party, but I don't know about Mom. I think a few big hits on the slots goes a long way."

Jimmy loves the idea of cruising to the game in Bryan's tiny black Toyota Camry. The car is a few years old now, but the radio more than makes up for the spartan interior. Today, the system is cranked up to twelve, just like when they were in high school. "Thanks for the lift. And for coming to the game." Bryan with his customary terse response, "Of course, bro."

The game comes and goes, as so many do in the cadence of summer. Uneventful, except for another summer evening playing ball. Jimmy's happy to play, to lace up his cleats and run around in the dirt for a few hours. Yup, one more summer in the sun.

Turning down First Street, Bryan lowers the volume. Mom's orders still stand after all these years. She never wants to *hear* them coming. The radio is playing EPMD's "Crossover", one of their favorite songs, only now bringing it down a few notches to a calmer level. The bass of the song still pulsing through their chests though, even at the half the max potential.

Approaching the house slowly, the Camry in full cruise mode. Bryan with his customary low slouch behind the wheel. Up ahead something blocks their usual clear path to the driveway. A shockwave of panic courses through both of the boys.

An ambulance, lights flashing, obstructing the driveway.

"What the…oh no." Bryan whispers under his breath. Though loud enough for Jimmy to hear. A small crowd of spectators gathering, milling around outside Mom's house. The summer sun still lighting the evening sky. Sunset approaching, but there's enough daylight left for the boys to have a full view of the growing horde.

Bryan hurriedly parks the car across the street, abruptly turning the car off with the windows still down. Both doors immediately swing open. The boys barreling out of the car and sprinting across the street heading straight towards Mom's house. Neither of them say a word. They don't need to.

Mom? Where the hell is Mom?

Both scan the crowd. Jimmy feeling a pang of regret in his stomach. Did that lunatic Slav finally do something to Mom? Because of the party? Sensing they should have never left her alone tonight.

Was Slav quiet last night waiting for revenge? Is that why he never called the cops? Oh damn. Mom? Where are you Mom… looking…somewhere…anywhere…

Finally, Jimmy finds Mom in crowd, standing with one of the other families from the row. She's in the driveway, blocked behind a few other neighbors. Thank goodness she's fine. "Bry, I got her. Over by the Wollack's."

Phew. Both boys let out a sigh of relief. But wait, then who's the ambulance for? Another quick scan. Jimmy sees everyone on the block appears accounted for.

In that moment, he glances up towards Mom's front door. Then, veering four feet to the left. The creaky hinges on Slav's filthy screen door swing open. The familiar sound of it slamming into his metal awning above. Two blue uniforms squeeze shoulder to shoulder backing out of the opening, initially obscuring what trails behind them. Each grunting loudly as they struggle to navigate the tight space. Then the object of their effort comes into Jimmy's view. The two paramedics are pulling a stretcher out of the house. A third member of the crew pushing hard at the other end.

A black body bag lays on top.

It takes all three first responders to maneuver the bulky piece of metal through the doorway. Jimmy freezes, standing near Mom in his baseball uniform, watching the surreal incident unfold. He stands out in the crowd— light grey vest with an "H" embroidered on the chest, royal blue t-shirt under with matching hat and socks that are pulled up to his knees. His pants are covered in dirt and blood, a result of his left knee gashing open following a slide at second base. Right now, though, he's oblivious to how he looks to others. Instead, fixating intently on the body bag as it exits the doorway. All other people drifting away from his field of vision.

The only sounds he hears are those of the stretcher on its procession to the waiting ambulance. Click, click, click, the sound of the wheels scraping each of the nine steps. The squeaking of the metal joints buckling under the weight of the bag's contents. The grinding and rumbling of the plastic wheels meeting concrete as the gurney rolls to the back of the transport. The groans of the paramedics as they lift the stretcher into the cabin. Doors slamming together, locking the stretcher inside. No more than two minutes pass until the funeral procession is complete.

Slav is gone.

Jimmy spent years imaging Slav's death. Sometimes even playing the role of vanquisher in an imaginary movie portraying the epic struggle of good versus evil. In life, in reality, that isn't to be the case. Slav is dead now. Not with the bang of a gun nor the villain befallen in some heroic clash, but with a whimper. The faint sound of one final breath.

Following the doors to the ambulance closing, a member of the paramedic team turns to Jimmy's family, all three of them gathered together now under the street light in front of the house: "We heard this guy was a bit of trouble. Well, he won't be bothering anyone again. I hope that helps." Two of the team members climb in the cab of the ambulance, driving away silently. No need for lights and sirens. The ambulance assumes the role of hearse.

The crowd continues to stand around once the medics leave, wandering almost aimlessly. Everyone talking with one another. The neighborhood beginning to buzz with the news of Slav's passing. A few folks venture into their homes, bringing out whatever beers or booze they have on hand. More people follow suit. Within minutes, an impromptu block party emerges. Music plays in front windows up and down the block, Bon Jovi and the obligatory Bruce Springsteen. A celebration erupts on First Street.

Ding dong, Slav is dead.

People laughing and smiling. They are all neighbors again.
Talking and greeting each other as if they are long lost friends
who serendipitously found each other. This is unlike anything
Jimmy witnessed before on the block. Turns out *everyone* was
terrified of Slav. The veil of fear finally lifting on the entirety
of the neighborhood.

An older woman who lives at the other end of the block
approaches the boys. "My, you boys are brave. You dealt with
so much from him." Jimmy had no idea other people knew what
was happening. Returning her comment with a befuddled look.
She then remorsefully admitted, "We all knew. We just didn't
know how to help."

"Thank you, ma'am. We appreciate you coming by now."
Bryan offers a solemn response.

Word spreads quickly downtown, with more people from the
surrounding blocks joining in on the festivities. Within a half
hour, the block is filled, the party growing exponentially. Jimmy
stands there soaking it all in. First Street engulfed in a swirl
of music, laughter, drinking and dancing. Just like the Irish
Luau the night before. Only he doesn't have the same feeling
of peace and joy.

Before leaving, the third paramedic recalls the scene inside
to one of the neighbors, a friend of his that is a local firefighter.
The conversation within earshot of Jimmy. The man is distraught.
Literally, his hands still shaking from his time inside Slav's
house. The hulking tattooed paramedic now reduced to tears.
Covering his mouth to prevent him from weeping aloud: "Holy
God. I never thought I would see something like that."

Never before experiencing such squalor and filth. He esti-
mates Slav was dead inside his house for about a week. His
bloated and decaying corpse adding to the weight of the transfer.
"His body was swollen. Face looked like it went through a meat

grinder. We found him upstairs, in a room right up there." The paramedic pointing to the bedroom in Slav's house that shares a wall with Jimmy's room.

The wretched smell trapped inside exacerbated by the oppressive summer heat. "All the windows were sealed shut, so the smell hit us as soon as we opened the door. Our one guy almost threw up immediately. We all went back to the bus to get masks. They didn't help much, though. Poor Tommy could barely keep his lunch in. Same with me."

The search leading them through the cluttered remains of a serial hoarder. "Everywhere we went, it got worse. Must be 30 years of magazines and newspapers in there. And that's not anywhere near the worst of it." Room after room producing another horrific scene. "He covered every mirror in feces. Rubbed it in by hand. The bathroom walls all green and black with mold and mildew. Urine stains all over the carpets and furniture. Rotted food with maggots in the garbage." Pausing, collecting himself, "You'd never know what kind of hell that place is from out here."

The paramedic squinting as he looks back towards Slav's house, shock setting into his being. Losing the color in his complexion, his eyes glassing over, continually blinking, trying to shake the memory from his mind. "That's no way for any human being to live. I'm telling you, man; I'll never forget today. Never." The paramedic's final words to his friend before departing.

Upon hearing the circumstances in which Slav lived, and ultimately died, Jimmy isn't much for celebrating. Relief? Absolutely. Despite how callous it may seem. However, Jimmy spent years visualizing what life was like on the other side of that plaster wall. Picturing his own home— comfortable, safe, clean, just with a madman screaming, singing and pounding his fists relentlessly.

Never once imagining how horrible life was like *inside* those walls. "You would never know what kind of hell that place is..." A different feeling comes over him entirely. Something he wasn't quite expecting when this day finally arrived.

Sadness.

He feels for Slav. *For Slav?* Through it all, Slav was a human being living in subhuman conditions on the other side of that wall. Yes, this is sadness. Grief. Even for Slav.

A person, regardless of how he lived and treated others, that was just carried out of his own home in a plain black body bag. No family to notify. No friends to alert of his passing. Just gone. Alone in the back of an ambulance.

Jimmy doesn't feel now is the time to celebrate, laugh or sing. Why would anyone celebrate the death when they didn't celebrate the life? Instead he just wants to go inside. He knows it will be quiet inside. For the first time in a long, *long* time, he knows it will be quiet inside. Perhaps it's the best way to celebrate the end of their journey together.

Finally, peace and quiet. For both of them.

Jimmy stays that way for the rest of the night. No TV, no conversation. Just resting in silence.

In the months following, Slav's house is cleared and sanitized of all remnants belonging to its longest tenured occupant. A new family moves in. A young couple, newly married. Life beginning anew in the townhouses on First Street. Slav's life ended. Taking with him the lesson that the only certainty in life is uncertainty.

But does he truly have more to offer than that?

All Is Not What It Seems

16

WALKING TOGETHER ON THE WINDING PATH, JOE
AND JIMMY PASS UNDER WEEPING WILLOWS AND
TOWERING FIR TREES. THE LITTLE LEAGUE COMPLEX
TO THEIR IMMEDIATE RIGHT, A NEW PLAYGROUND
RESEMBLING A PIRATE SHIP TO THEIR LEFT. THE
WARMTH OF THE AFTERNOON SUN IS AT ITS APEX.

The thaw in the air fully removed, along with the thaw in the
conversation. Jimmy realizing life lessons provide the reference
guide for us as we continue along her corridors of wisdom.

Jimmy pauses the dialogue, offering momentary silence to
acknowledge Slav. Gratitude for the lesson. Both men walk a
bit lighter now. Eager to unearth whatever kernels of knowledge
are left for them to squeeze out of the day. Time is growing
short. That much they both know.

"Those were wild times, weren't they, Joe?"

"That's one way to put it, sure."

"I don't get it, though. Why do you keep coming back to Slav?
That's a memory long gone by now. Same as him."

"Really? Is that so. Just a memory?"

"Of course it is. What else is there? Do you want me to feel bad for him or something? To reconcile with the years of threats and rage he battered my family with, to *repent*?"

"No. That's not it. I believe you hold no ill will towards the man."

At this point in time, Jimmy begins to question his entire time with Joe today. Are we really only going to talk about uncertainty and Slav? *Slav?* Of all people! Maybe the student finally equaling the teacher? Maybe there is no more knowledge left in this park. This Memory Lane come to life. "Alright, then why?" Jimmy presses the question further. Feeling a new level of stature in their relationship.

"The shadow of uncertainty."

"What?"

"Not what, *who*. And you don't know yet?"

"Quit it with the riddles and with quizzing me, please?"

Joe pauses. Deliberating his next move, is it right? Is now finally the time? Joe then cautiously answers Jimmy's question: "Because in the end, you saw Slav just as I knew him."

Jimmy snaps his head back towards Joe. Halting mid-step at the revelation. His face tells all. *WHAT* DID YOU JUST SAY? *Knew* him? Actually *knew* him?? Never in a million years did Jimmy expect to hear those words. Never.

Life truly is uncertain.

"Do you remember when your brother threw that party? The one that started everything off between your family and him?"

"Yes. I do."

"Do you also remember a time when Slav lived with his father?"

"Vaguely, I mean, I guess so."

"Well, Slav's father passed away shortly before that party. And that night was all he needed to direct his emotions away from the pain of losing someone he loved. And loved dearly."

Jimmy is still rocked by the news that Joe knew Slav, knew him, *Joe freaking knew him*. He doesn't know what to do next, what to say next. Standing there behind the Little League field, trying to process the new information. Jimmy's brain and emotions on full overload.

Realizing the gravity of his confession, Joe fills the silence next. "Now might be a good time for you to meet the Slav I knew. If you would, please allow me to tell you of *my* relationship with him."

"Please, Joe. Please do." Shock, disappointment and a tinge of anger all rolling together. Jimmy's mind spinning at the revelation. Joe *knew* him. Like he knows me?

Joe's story with Slav begins long before Jimmy came to know either man.

Continuing to walk the path, Joe takes the bend left, the magnitude of the Bayonne Bridge casting a shadow over them. Before speaking, though, Joe gathers himself, drawing in a deep breath, focusing his gaze. Something Jimmy is wholly unaccustomed to witnessing in his mentor.

Joe begins speaking in a melancholy tone. For seemingly the first time ever, refusing to make eye contact with Jimmy, instead trading glances between the sky and the ground. Arms down to his sides, his hands connecting around his lower back, linked together by his leather book.

Solemn. A reverent bow of his head.

The story unfolds straight from the chambers of Joe's heart. "Slav spent nearly his entire life in that house. Moving in when he was a child, around the same age as when you and I first met. He and his father. Two men on an adventure together. It was an exciting time for him. Finally moving into a house of their own. Excited it was across from a park.

They moved from their cramped one-bedroom apartment in

midtown Bayonne, where Slav slept on a fold away cot in the living room. In this home, he would have a bedroom of his own and all the green grass a boy could hope for. Slav believed his future was bright. His dreams finally coming true. From time to time, throughout his childhood, I would find him walking the streets and around this very park. He had a few friends, but they weren't close. Not like you and the boys. Slav was simply a boy looking to find his way. In the park. And in life.

Sound familiar?

We talked together many times and formed a bond over the intervening years. As Slav made his way along the path from adolescence to young adulthood. It was never easy for him to make, let alone keep, friends. I was different for him, though, just letting him be himself."

Joe serving as one of the neighborhood nice guys. Always.

Jimmy confounded at the story. The striking parallels, feeling as though he could understand what Slav was feeling in those moments of his youth. The boundless excitement to cross the street and enter into the park. An invisible threshold into a magical world of adventure and freedom.

Joe continues with the narrative, bringing to light the depths of darkness within Slav. "As our relationship grew closer, he would confide in me about his home life as well. I appreciated him opening up. It wasn't easy for him, but he was very brave, and I would often feel called to remind him of that.

You see, he loved his father very much. Enjoying every moment of their time together. His role model in every way. Idolizing him, in fact. His father worked for the local oil refinery, the one at the end of the block on the other side of the bridge. You remember it, don't you?" Joe pointing to the underpass of the bridge, the refinery long gone now. Shut down sometime during Jimmy's childhood. It's the one that gave birth to The

Burning Man.

"His father earned a living the hard way. Grinding through every day in difficult conditions. Long shifts and little pay. Slav wanted to be just like his father when he grew up. Wanted to earn an honest living with his hands. He thought it was honorable profession. Especially since his father was respected as a 'working man' in the neighborhood. His dad wasn't some suit, and the men at The Steel Arches loved him for it. 'Salt of the Earth' they would say about him.

Slav was the apple that didn't *want* to fall far from the tree. Only Slav's father was a far cry from any role model a boy could, and certainly *should*, have in life. In time, he confided in me something no one else knew. His truth. That his father tormented him. Day after day. From the moment he woke up to the moment he fell asleep, even beyond. In the dark hours of the night, waking him from a deep slumber with whispers of how he owned him. Scratching a knife against his bedpost. How Slav's only purpose in life was to respect his father.

As a child, constantly tell him he was fat. Ridiculing the food he ate, even though his father was the one that decided what the boy would eat. Telling him he was a loser with no friends. Even though his father forbade him to play with other kids. Discouraging playing sports in this very park because 'he wasn't going to make it anyway'. He was stupid. Useless.

Slav suffered a relentless assault from the time he was a very young boy, his father's verbal lashings serving as his earliest memories.

Some days were worse. His father waking him out of deep sleep with a bucket of cold water, berating him that he was nothing but a lazy dog. Why couldn't he get up and work hard like his old man? His father then telling him dogs are meant to be kicked and beaten if they were lazy. 'That's the only way they learn.' He would say. So, the way he treated Slav would be no different. Kicking him and slapping him as he rolled his youthful frame out of bed at 5 a.m. 'Time for your walk' his father would say. Then grabbing him by the neck, leading him to the bathroom and forcing him to urinate next to the toilet, only so Slav would be obligated to clean it up before breakfast. That way the smell would linger in his food.

His father mocking his slow reading. Rolling up the newspaper or magazine when he fumbled the words and beating him with it because of his failure to learn. Bloody nose. Bloody lip. Time and time again.

Cruel words continuing to accompany the beatings: stupid, fat, slow, disgusting, useless.

Slav grew so scared of his father he would cower in the corner of his bedroom and urinate on himself at the mere sound of his father walking upstairs. 'See,' his father would say 'just like a dog, peeing on the carpet.'

Slav's mistakes were always punished. Whipped with extension cords. Doused with alcohol or paint thinner. Minor transgressions, such as yawning during one his father's embellished stories of greatness, or father's coffee in the morning not being hot enough, usually meant kneeling in kitty litter bins filled with dry rice.

More egregious infractions, such as failing to clean up his father's plate or not having a drink ready after his shift, meant forcing Slav to kneel in those same kitty litter bins filled with rusty nails and screws. Time would drag slowly during those punishments. Slav left with nothing but silence and pain.

Father is to be respected. Always.

As Slav grew into a man, his father turned his attention to absolutely destroying what little of Slav's self-worth remained. What woman would ever love such a pathetic creature? Who in their right mind would ever love such a disgusting mutt of human being? His father once kicking him with his steel tipped boot so hard in his midsection, Slav was nearly hospitalized. Leaving him unable to walk for a week.

'I want to make sure nothing like you ever comes from this Earth again.'

In order to eat, his father requiring Slav to list why he is grateful. Spitting on him and slapping him while he waited for Slav to recite the verses. He was *lucky* to have his Dad. Without his father, he would be nothing, a nobody. His father was the one that *cared* for him. Provided for him. His father was *kind* enough to let him live with him. His father's *honest* work supported his fat, lazy, stupid, worthless son. His father *let* him live with him far past the time when any child should be living with his parents.

'At least a dog dies after ten years,' his father would say. 'It's a damn shame you're still here.'

Slav grew afraid to shower because when he took his clothes off his father ridiculed his obese body. Looking in the mirror only reinforcing the shame. When he chose clothes different than those his father selected, he was chastised for making his own decisions. Conditioned from the outset of his life that father knows best. Always.

Slav knew nothing but abuse nearly from the moment he entered this world. But most especially from the moment he moved into that house. It was an evil den of torment shattering the dreams of the life he envisioned. For all intents and purposes, Slav was someone the world would consider living a worthless life. As he would often say to me, 'If your own dad believes you're worthless, then isn't that what you are?'"

Joe pauses as he speaks that single, powerful question. The details are sickening. Jimmy stands before him heartbroken.

He doesn't recall much of Slav's father at all. Thankfully. Always thinking Slav himself was the monster. Never before considering the origins of his behavior. That maybe the apple didn't fall far from the tree.

The story of Slav's life hits Jimmy deeply. All of the threats that Slav made over the years: castration, servitude, the midnight whispers. They all came from somewhere. Or someone. With sorrow enveloping Jimmy's words, he asks, "How come you never told me this before?"

"Because that was Slav's story. His life. Not yours. Well, at least it wasn't at the time."

"If you knew all of this, then what happened between the two of you?"

"I'll tell you." Joe resumes Slav's tale. Jimmy valiantly trying to make sense of it all. "Slav's father passed away suddenly, or at least to Slav it was. Though it was hardly a surprise death to anyone else, given the way the man lived. However, for Slav, his father's death was something he didn't consider possible. He never, *never* saw it coming. In his eyes, his father was immortal. Then, suddenly, without warning, the man who controlled every action in his life, controlled every decision, every thought was gone. Everything changed. Slav's entire world changed in an instant. Forever."

Joe turning towards Jimmy, their eyes connecting. Wanting what he would disclose next to resonate deeply within the student. Jimmy at full attention as they continue onwards together. The sights and sounds surrounding them fading. His single point of focus drawn to each word of the tale.

"I would find him walking, muttering to himself. Angry. Afraid. Depressed. I would provide a kind word. A reminder he wasn't alone in this world. Letting him know I was there to help. There for him. That this was a difficult time, but he didn't have to go through it alone.

He would lash out and interrupt me when I spoke. Accusing me of wanting his father to pass. I would respond by sending food or new clothes to his house. Anything to show him that someone in the world cared for him. He threw it all in the trash. Told me I was trying to 'mess his mind'. Began threatening me. I didn't back down; sending more food, clothes, blankets, letters, cards. Anything to get the message through that he was not alone. I was afraid of what would happen to him. For weeks, I continued unconditionally."

Jimmy, hanging on every word, each sentence opening a world he never knew existed. The world right next door. A singular question coming to mind: "Joe, I don't get it. Something *must* have happened. You don't exactly leave people behind." An ever so slight sniffle preceding his response, "Well, remember that party your brother threw?"

"Oh no," Jimmy thinking to himself, "did *we* screw this up?"

"Let me explain, before you get yourself all out of sorts." Joe immediately picking up on Jimmy's angst. "We were walking in the park one day, on a different path than this, speaking about the party. He was angry, outright hostile. Focusing solely on what you did *to* him. How offended he was. And what he was going to do about it. I explained to him that he had a choice to make of how to respond. The choice to be himself and not to be his father. The choice to now live *his* life."

Jimmy gingerly questioning, "So what did he say to that? Or do we already know that answer?" Joe immediately acknowledges the question and responds, "I pressed him. Believing there was good inside him. That he just needed to let his light shine. For once in his life I wanted *him* to see it. To *feel* it."

"Then what?"

"He finally told me the truth."

"About what?"

"Not what, who." Joe pauses before continuing. "You." Jimmy is floored by the statement. A fleeting pause before Joe shares the details, "With his father gone, he no longer revered him. Instead, he idolized *you*. You were the boy he always wished he could be. Living out what he dreamt his life to look like. Free. Playful. Fearless. Surrounded by friends and family. Full of life. *Full of joy*. Someone he believed deep within that he would *never* be."

Jimmy's hands begin to shake, eyes watering. Confusion, accompanied with a slight sense of resentment, welling up within in his body. "I don't get it, Joe. Why? Why did he act that way towards us, then?"

"I know this is confusing, but please try to understand his point of view. The way he spoke to you is the only form of communication Slav ever experienced. He believed very strongly that his father loved him dearly. So, screams and threats became his language of love. Unfortunately, he never learned to speak from his heart. Never learned to speak with kindness. Do you see now?"

Jimmy responding forcefully, gripped with emotion, "Why didn't you save him, then? Why did you let him destroy himself?"

"His life was not mine to save. It was *his* to save." Joe elaborates further, "We stayed close despite the strife in the years after his father passed. He was making progress, starting to even have goals and dreams for his own life. That's why when you initially came to me, I knew he would never harm you or your family. However, as with all journeys through life, he came to the point that in order to move forward, more was required. Much more, unfortunately, than Slav was willing to bear. He chose a different path. That's when the white Cadillac appeared."

"What was he so afraid of that he stopped?" Jimmy pleading to rewrite history.

"Not what. Who."

"Who then? Who could stop him then?"

"The only person that could. Himself."

Joe let the words linger as they found a home in Jimmy's heart. "You see, Slav may have been abused by his father, but he was tortured by the thoughts inside his head long after the man was gone. His struggle raging between the courage to face those thoughts and the work to change how he viewed himself, the world, life. The battle between what was required to light the day or to succumb to the shadows of anger, self-loathing and fear. Two roads diverged in a wood, as the poem says. I offered the one less traveled by. His choice made all the difference."

"But why, why now? Why is this important now? So long after the moment is gone?" Jimmy pleading to comprehend. Eyes glassy and cheeks red.

Placing a gentle hand on Jimmy's left shoulder, Joe speaks definitively, "Because the true impact of our lives is not measured by how brightly we shine our own light. Rather, it is found in our openness to see the light in others and in guiding them so they, too, may shine brightly. One light may dominate the day, but it pales in comparison to the brilliant perfection of all the stars shining in the night sky."

Joe, again letting his words rest on Jimmy's ears, and in his heart, before explaining further, "Impact is found even in some-one like Slav. Someone whom the world treated as inconse-quential, ultimately discarded like a piece of garbage in a black plastic bag. In truth, his impact is far greater than you, and many, would ever realize."

Jimmy stands speechless. "Slav? But how?" Head spinning with confusion. There has to be meaning in all of this. *Has* to be.

Joe then details the unseen: "I was there that day, too. The summer evening he was carried out of his house. A witness to the crude funeral procession down his front steps." Jimmy flashes to the moment in his mind. Recalling with vivid detail his every move, every thought. "And I saw you there, too. Dirt and blood-stained uniform, still playing the game hard if I recall correctly. One more summer in the sun as it were. You were left standing there, surrounded by people celebrating. They were shaking hands, laughing, singing, spreading cheers as if they had slayed the mighty beast themselves."

The flood of memories washes over Jimmy. He can feel everything Joe says. As if sent back in time, witnessing the moment from across the street, outside of his body, seated on the hood of the parked black Camry. A bizarre sensation overcoming him.

"But then I watched as Slav taught you his final, and most profound, lesson." Jimmy shaking, still lost in a fog of memories, emotions. The new reality of a life, Slav's life, and now his life. Everything he understood before today permanently shifting. "In that moment, you felt for him. Despite the dreadful nature of your relationship, in the end, you saw who you always wanted to see. You did not sit in judgement for how he lived his life, the choices he made that ultimately consumed his body and his mind." Joe speaks slowly, purposefully, allowing the power of his words to sow deep within Jimmy's soul. "And because of you, finally, in death, Slav experienced something that eluded him all his life."

"What?" Jimmy whispers. Barely audible. The weight of the Joe's words continually landing forcefully. Wave upon wave crashing inside him.

"Grace."

A moment passes before Joe expounds on the simple and powerful word. Illuminating the experience. "You see, your innate response was not to see the flaws that pervaded the man next door. Instead, when his final moment came and others chose to celebrate death as the conclusion of something terrible, you shined a peaceful light to celebrate the beauty of a life."

Jimmy is immediately overwhelmed with emotion. He wants it to stop. He wants to call Quinn. He wants to go home. "What is this all about? Why did I take this path? I didn't need to know this. I didn't." Begging, pleading, the gravity of the words weighing him down.

Responding with comfort and compassion, Joe steadies himself in front of Jimmy, meeting him face to face on the path. "Yes, you did need to know this. Because you were meant to be here, now, in this moment. Here so that you could become who you were meant to be. Every single part of your life, Slav included, has happened *for* you. Every. Single. One."

Jimmy gathers himself as the words hang in the air. EVERY. SINGLE. ONE.

Following several moments, Jimmy regains his composure, still unsure of what exactly is happening. Standing tall in front of his mentor, Joe speaks directly to Jimmy's soul now. "And now, there is one person you must offer the same divine grace you granted Slav all those years ago." Sniffling. Eyes bloodshot, a few tears drying on Jimmy's cheeks as his stance mirrors Joe's. Whispering softly towards his mentor. "Who?" Straightening his gaze, Joe steels his hazel eyes to meet Jimmy's. The window to the student's soul cast wide open.

"You."

SECTION FIVE

Grace Comes Home

The Road Less Traveled

17

The word lingers in the air. Searching for a place to land, to call home.

You.

Suspended in time, drifting directly towards Jimmy's heart. He is no longer crying. Resolve steadying his posture. Jimmy's eyes look towards Joe. Wiping away the remaining tears. "What do you mean, me?" Sensing something much deeper coming on the horizon.

"Tell me kid, how do you experience joy?"

"Absolutely. Happy to. My family. Quinn and the kids. Traveling and experiencing new places, people."

"I asked about you," Joe immediately follows.

"I'm grateful, Joe. Lucky to be blessed with my family, those moments together. Their love. That's what brings me joy."

"Ah, luck. Is that it? You found the pot of gold at the end of the rainbow? And it's filled with joy?"

Jimmy responds sternly, "What are you getting at?" The roller coaster of emotions steadily climbs back from shock, sadness and sorrow.

"And how does it feel to be so lucky? Are you proud of it? Basking in the virtue of your good fortune." Jimmy tilts his head, he does not like the direction of the conversation. Notably because he feels directionless in the moment. "Get to the point, please. Enough dancing around. You said I had to show myself grace. For what?" Frustration visibly setting in.

"Because of the cross you feel compelled to bear. The one you alone see. Without releasing that burden, you will never truly experience joy. Never truly experience who you were meant to be." Cross? Compelled?? Confusion reigns supreme, only now combining with wrath for a potentially volatile cocktail of emotions. A hallmark of their time together all those years ago.

Jimmy stands there in the middle of the asphalt path. Statuesque. The Little League behind them now. The Bayonne Bridge hovering above to their right. Having rounded a circular path while speaking about Slav's life.

He doesn't know whether to walk away or to punch Joe in the face at the most recent suggestion. "Cross I bear. That's garbage." Feeling as he did all those years ago standing in front of Mr. Bexton. The smell of the old man's toxic breath coming back again. The sinking feeling of being chastised.

Burden? For what, having a good life? Jimmy worked hard for it: single parent house, lunatic neighbor, doubters, haters, even during corporate life. On and on the list goes until he becomes silent. Unsure how to proceed answering the question, though now sure he isn't going to leave or react poorly. That happened once. He is not doing it again.

"No answer to how it feels to be so lucky then?" Joe quizzes him.

"I don't understand what burden I'm supposed to carry."

"I never said you were 'supposed to'."

Joe presses the matter further. "Tell me, is your life worth celebrating?" Jimmy closes his eyes. Yet another wave of emotion crashes inside him, a thunderous gut punch. What's

Joe driving at?

Joe presses harder still. Sensing an opportunity to shine a light into a dark crevasse of Jimmy's life. The questions now coming fast and furious. "Tell me, how does it feel when your children sing 'Happy Birthday' to *you*? When they decorate a birthday cake just for *you*? Hang decorations for a party to celebrate *you*? How about date night with Quinn? Your anniversary? Celebrating the special moments of *your* life together. Tell me, please. How do they feel *for you*?"

Remaining silent. Jimmy absorbs the verbal pounding. The emotions cascading inside him: anger, resentment, fear. An internal tempest raging. His body feels ragged.

"Go ahead, kid. Tell me. Or better yet, how do you feel taking pictures on your family vacations, at the beach building sand castles? At the theme parks, having breakfast with your children and their favorite characters?" Joe speaking as if he lives in their house. How could he possibly know all of this? "*Their* joy is real. Their soul shines through in every moment. What about yours?"

"Knock it off, Joe." Blood in the water. Like Kermit and the boys on the Pony League field. History repeating itself.

"No. It's time."

"What the hell do you want me to say?"

"The truth."

Jimmy inhales a deep, deep breath. His diaphragm expanding. The raging tempest starts to clear. Another breath. Another clearing. Is light finally beginning to break through? Jimmy lets the negative emotions go. The fear, anger, confusion. Releasing them.

Perhaps there is another lesson today.

One more deep breath. One more clearing. Finally, Jimmy speaks. Quietly, but assuredly. "You're right, Joe. I never feel

I deserve those moments— the birthday cake, the anniversary, the vacations. I always feel those moments are meant for some-one else."

Interjecting, Joe asks, "And why don't *you* deserve to feel that joy too?" Jimmy begins to well up, his internal emotions brimming to the surface. He knows the answer. It's something he's heard countless times over the years.

"Because I'm just lucky to be alive."

The interrogation ceases. The verbal body blows halt, serving their intended purpose. Light breaks through to the dark recesses of Jimmy's emotional vault. The words meet the air, Jimmy finally says aloud what he's repeated in his mind thousands of times before: *just lucky to be alive.* And as he does, an anvil lifts off his chest. His face softens. His eyes, still watery, grow warm again.

"The truth helps, doesn't it?" Joe asks, already knowing the answer.

"It does. I just always thought that's how I was supposed to feel. It's what everyone told me for years. What I told myself."

"I understand. Come, sit with me. There are two more people that I would like you to meet. Just remember, please, that forgiveness often accompanies grace."

The two men continue their journey again, following as the path leads past the Bayonne Bridge and then back again along the water. The sun now beginning to set behind the bridge. It's amber rays of the twilight 'golden hour' casting two long shadows behind them as they walk.

Joe points ahead to a bench, "Let's have a seat, shall we?" Jimmy's eyes wander ahead, spotting their end point. The bench faces the water, the back turned away from the path and the nearby children's playground, nestled near a fir tree.

Joe's bench. Jimmy knows it immediately. Spending hours upon hours there during his youth talking, learning, growing. It's the perfect place to experience the sun setting on the western horizon beyond the bridge. A natural spotlight beaming through the immense steel arches, illuminating their intended destination.

The men sit down, assuming their traditional spots. Joe on the left, Jimmy on the right-hand side.

As he sits, Joe removes his cap and places it on top of his book in the space between them. He inhales slowly and deeply, then reaches his right hand into his coat pocket. Where is this going? Jimmy unsure he can handle another surprise. Immediately telling himself: trust him. Just trust him. Like the first time they sat on this bench together decades ago.

Joe pulls out a small brown leather pouch, rattling as it settles into his sturdy palm. He pulls the tiny drawstring open, pouring seven stones into his left palm. His massive, calloused hand morphing into a tender cradle. An offering to his seatmate: "Choose two. One for each hand," Joe says, glancing from the stones towards Jimmy.

A mineral rainbow borne out in the palm of Joe's hand: red, orange, yellow, green, blue, indigo and violet. A smooth polish accentuates the beauty of the marvelous stones. They are roughly the size of a large marble, each holding their natural shape. Jimmy instinctively grasps the green and violet stones, taking one in each hand. Following as instructed. "What is this, Joe?" The question riddled with apprehension.

"The road less traveled."

The Choice to Fly

18

IMMEDIATELY, HEAT BEGINS TO GENERATE IN EACH OF JIMMY'S CLENCHED FISTS. AS IF THE STONES ABSORB THE INTENSITY OF HIS EMOTIONS, MAGNIFYING THEM. HANDS PULSING. WHAT IS HAPPENING HERE?

Trust him. Just trust him. "Close your eyes," Joe softly instructs. Jimmy obliges, gently shutting his eyelids. Slowing his breath. Joe's calm voice receiving Jimmy's full attention. "It's time to go back to the Tuesday morning. To go back to September 11th. To go back to the Towers." The stones throb. Gathering additional heat and energy from Jimmy, from the vision emerging in his mind's eye. Passing back through time. A blurred tunnel before him. White and gray shadows emerging. The image gaining color and clarity with each methodical inhale and exhale.

For years, Jimmy opposing the idea of looking back. Now, it's the only way forward.

Finding himself tensing as the vision unfolds.

The details, vibrant and realistic, begin to filter into focus. The bright sunshine and clear skies of that Tuesday morning. Wincing as he looks upwards at the powder blue sky as he crosses West Street to the office. Seeing himself dressed for the day ahead. Tan dress pants, blue gingham shirt, brown leather shoes. Brand new silver flip-phone in his left pocket. Settling in at his desk inside the team's conference room. Turning on his computer. Alone.

The roaring engine overhead, the first plane barreling into the North Tower. The calm response from the executive at the desk nearest the window: "Guess we'll find out soon enough." Calling Quinn. Her worried voice imploring him to leave if it wasn't safe. "I will. Promise." Back to the window again. The jumper.

Dear God. The jumper. All over again.

Laboring so hard for so long to block this moment from his mind. Suppressing the scene while driving life forward. Each day spent in a high-rise office building a quiet reminder of the jumper. For years, constantly striving to push the image deeper into darkness. Now, here he is again. Jumping. Falling towards his final resting place. The twisted body on the blood-stained roof. Jimmy recalling his thought from that day: the man had no way home. His eyes grip tighter. Beginning to cry for the man, the jumper. All over again.

"Open your eyes." Joe's tender voice requests. Jimmy obliges. Brushing away a tear or two. "Now, please, tell me what you see," Joe calmly states.

Jimmy recounts his vision to Joe. The details of the day. The beginning of the attacks. Not knowing what was coming next. The fear. Then the jumper. The man on the window ledge with no way home. Wiping away a few more tears as he recounts the memory.

"He had no way home."

"Close your eyes again," Joe's instructs gently. The stones gathering heat once again. Vibrating to the rhythm of Jimmy's heart. Instantly, the jumper appears on the ledge. Only this time, Jimmy can *feel* him. Feel his pain. Feel his anguish. As if he is standing next to him. Feeling the *choice* the jumper has to make, to turn around and face the flames, the smoke and certain death inside the building.

Or to fly?

Either choice leading to the same outcome. *The only choice is how.*

The jumper left for work that beautiful morning, excited for the start of the day. His life seemingly only beginning; love, family, friends. His cherished moments growing exponentially. The wonderful promise of what is to come in his life. Never for a moment did he consider that today is the last day of his life. All of our choices do, indeed, ultimately lead to the same ending. And today is his last series of choices.

Jimmy stops crying as his eyes are closed. Something different overcoming him entirely. But what?

"Open your eyes," Joe's kind voice requests. "Please, tell me what you see." Jimmy recounts his new experience with the jumper. Fear no longer holding sway. Beginning to understand what is happening in the moment. Telling Joe the *feeling* of what is happening. The jumper has a choice. And he chooses to fly.

"Close your eyes. This time open your heart."

Eyes closing. Heat collecting. Instantly, Jimmy finds himself back at the window near the executive's desk in the World Financial Center. Standing there fixated on the North Tower across the street. Scanning the wall of windows of the giant tower. Finding the jumper again.

This time not only seeing him make the decision. Jimmy experiences it with him. The jumper deciding to fly. I understand why. Jimmy finally gains comfort in the choice. No longer afraid for the man. No tears. Instead peace presides. I understand your choice. You are meant to fly.

As the jump begins again something happens. An image appears that is beyond his understanding.

In the sky above, amidst the smoke and falling debris, a river of light between the worlds of man and spirit emerges. Resplendent light, a shimmering golden stream, shines directly on the jumper once in flight. A brief moment later the gilded brilliance engulfs the jumper, elevating his spirit from his body, enmeshing his soul with the current flowing from an endless source. All the while, the transient vessel that served his life so well completes its journey to the roof below.

An angel is born.

Tears stream down Jimmy's cheeks as he is seated next to Joe, eyes firmly closed, witnessing the vision. The stones heat now pulsate through his entire being. Each heartbeat dispersing the intensity throughout Jimmy's body.

The sight is beyond words. Pure. Divine.

The jumper chose to fly. And his spirit continues to fly. Travelling upwards in union with the light, protecting others after his physical body fell to its end. Guiding his loved ones and teaching others there is great power in the choice to fly. Teaching Jimmy.

An angel was born that day. An angel born amidst unspeakable tragedy. Light somehow finding a way to penetrate even the darkest of days.

"Open your eyes." Joe's tender voice interrupting the beauty of the vision. Jimmy inhales deeply. A feeling of peace permeates his being. The heat of the stones cooling to their natural state.

The fear, anguish, and ire towards the jumper dissipate. Understanding the depth and force of that moment is uplifting.

There is *beauty* in that moment. There is *beauty* in that experience. Shedding no tears this time while recounting the story to Joe. Instead, speaking humbly, grateful for witnessing a miracle.

"We are surrounded by miracles each and every day," Joe states calmly. "What matters is how we look at the world around us. As we said, shining a light on the shadow of uncertainty means sometimes we have to be willing to shine a light into that darkness. And at other times, *be* the light."

Even the stones in Jimmy's hands feel lighter. Filled with air instead of raw matter. The sensation in his arms, chest, and head all similarly buoyant. "Thank you for showing me that," Jimmy graciously responds.

"I didn't show you anything. You found the way yourself." Joe replies. "Well, either way, thank you." Jimmy again offers.

"We aren't done yet, kid." Raising his eyebrows and tilting his head sideways, Jimmy shakes off the fog in his head and brings himself back to the present moment. What more could possibly happen after that? "Okay then. What's next?" Jimmy asking, almost cheerfully.

"Not what. *Who.* I said there were two people you needed to meet."

A Simple Smile

19

JIMMY CONTINUING TO HOLD THE STONES IN HIS HANDS, GRIPPING THEM LOOSELY, HIS FINGERTIPS ROLLING OVER THEIR SMOOTH SURFACE. THE CONTOURS ENGRAINED IN HIS MIND. THEIR SUBTLE FORCE CONTINUES EXPANDING BEYOND HIS HANDS, PULSATING THROUGH HIS ARMS, CHEST, LEGS, TOES, EVEN THE CROWN OF HIS HEAD. ENERGY RADIATING DEEP INTO HIS BEING.

What *is* all this?

Before introducing Jimmy to the second person, Joe expounds on Jimmy's experience: "Life provides the lessons. *We* provide the perspectives. And fear is often a powerful force shaping perspective, masquerading as adages, certainty, luck. However, the path taken in search of the truth, *the absolute truth*, reveals to us something far more powerful than fear. For in truth, we aren't meant to merely survive; rather, we are meant to *thrive*. To be free in all of our brilliant light, ever impacting the lives we encounter. Ever connected."

Jimmy answers meekly. "I'm trying to follow. Honestly, I am, Joe. But I'm in awe of what just happened." Still confounded from his encounter with the jumper.

"What just happened?" Joe asks, as if he's unaware of what just transpired. "You know, the jumper, the angel, how everything changed."

"Did it? Or were you able to change your perspective on what happened? That way you could see who was truly in front of you the entire time." Joe continues, "You let go of the fear surrounding his death, of how it reflects upon your own life experience. Of any resentment or judgement towards him not wanting to fight to return to his family. Instead, you chose to see him with love, with light. Which finally allowed you to see his true self."

"I understand. I *felt* it." Excitement coursing through Jimmy.

"Felt what?"

A single word springing to mind. "*Love*."

A wide grin appears on Joe's face that exact moment. Working to contain his elation as he speaks. "Yes. Loving someone means wanting their spirit to soar and their light to shine. As you do with Quinn, your children, and now, the jumper. It wasn't that he had to fight to return home. In that moment, it was simply time for the angel inside to fly again, to return to our natural home and embark on a different path and purpose."

The two men sit silent on the park bench for a few moments afterwards. Jimmy quietly recalls the day's discussion. Replaying the events in his mind: The truth about the apple tree. And choices. The truth about life. And uncertainty. The truth about Slav. And grace. Now the truth about the jumper. And choosing to fly.

Finally, Jimmy speaks. Soft words emanating from the depth of his soul. The calm of understanding now taking hold in his body. "Now what?" Empowered with the day's education about truth, yet physically exhausted by the sheer emotion of it all.

"Like I said before, not what, who. Let's meet the second person, shall we?"

The Walk to the Other Side

20

JOE ADJUSTS HIMSELF ON THE PARK BENCH, STRAIGHTENING HIS SPINE AND FOCUSING HIS GAZE OUT ON THE WATER, THE LAPPING WAVES GENTLY BREAKING ON THE SHORE UNDER THE SETTING SUN.

"Close your eyes, and take your walk to the ferry." Jimmy immediately knows where they were going next. And who he is going to meet. Given how far they've traveled together, both in life and today, this isn't a moment for hesitation.

Go all the way. See what's on the other side.

Jimmy closes his eyes. The stones begin to warm. Vibrating again in rhythm with the beat of his heart. No hazy imagery this time, Jimmy instead immediately flashes to standing outside the World Financial Center. Quickly grasping his surroundings and his next move. Only this time, confidently moving towards the marina. Certain of how this vision will end. The ferry home is just on the other side. Just one person to see. Knowing who he will meet in the middle.

The smiling man.

The embodiment of pure evil living in Jimmy's mind for eighteen years. There *is* evil in the world. Anywhere. Everywhere. We are surrounded by its potential. Be cautious. Tread carefully. Jimmy's witnessed it firsthand. Malevolence personified. Hate smiling at you.

He visually recounts the slow walk to the ferry. Seeing the man again, smiling, the Cheshire grin from ear to ear. His rich tan skin enriching the intensity of the white smile. Again, Jimmy doesn't stop to speak. Even in his mind's eye, he can't bear to stop. Is it because he doesn't have the time? Or the courage?

"You can open your eyes now." Joe whispers softly. Jimmy opens them, reluctantly. No magic this time. No reawakening. Wanting to go back in to search for the truth.

Please ask me to close my eyes again, Joe. *Please.* How far is he willing to go to find the truth? How deep inside is he willing to go? "Okay, then. Close your eyes again." Good. Let's find the truth.

The stones transport Jimmy back to the marina. Right where he *wants* to be. The heat intensifying, stones vibrating in his palms. The scene begins to unfold again, same as before. Something is coming, though. Jimmy senses it. Or perhaps someone.

Finding himself again locking eyes with the smiling man. That wicked grin greeting him once again. This time, though, the internal movie changes. The scene stops. As if the projector has failed, and the reel is preventing it from resuming its duty. All of the commotion surrounding the two men— fires, evacuation, debris, emergency personnel— comes to a complete halt.

Time stands still.

"What now?" Jimmy whispers under his breath in the external world, his eyes clutching tighter still. Joe faintly hearing the comment. As if by sheer willpower, something startling happens next.

The smiling man speaks first.

In lieu of a dark, sadistic tone, Jimmy is greeted by a warm, temperate sound. The man's voice is inviting, as if it is one Jimmy's heard a million times before. "Whose voice is that?" Another whisper barely audible for Joe. The voice is embracing in every way imaginable. Caring.

The smiling man's voice feels like home. "Would you like to know who I am?" He doesn't sound evil. How could this be possible? I *know* he is evil. Jimmy, stuck in the moment, astonished even, inside the vision of his mind, is still unable to speak a single word. Simply nodding "yes" in response. What he hears next shocks him to his very core.

"I am the Angel of Death. Here to welcome all the souls home. To provide them comfort in their journey to the other side." Jimmy begins to weep outside of his vision. Deep, remorseful tears. Sobbing heavily at the revelation. Joe sits ardently by his friend's side, moved to tears himself as he witnesses the impact of the vision on Jimmy.

Another angel?

Inside the waking dream, Jimmy remains motionless in stunned silence. Absorbing the Angel of Death's words, never saying anything in return. A moment passes, the movie reel begins again. Jimmy is compelled to move. Silently turning his back to the man, the angel, proceeding forward to the ferry. Glancing over his shoulder several times as he walks. Each time, he locks eyes with the stranger, the Angel of Death, and receives a smile in return.

To welcome the souls *home*? The light of truth revealed. The smiling man, the very physical embodiment of evil persisting in his mind for so long, is instead providing solace for the dying. An angel stands at the base of the burning towers, there to guide the souls that would perish that morning. To ease their pain and fear as their time on earth ends so abruptly. Despite being surrounded by bloodshed, the man does not fear death. Because he *is* death.

Continuing in his mind's eye, Jimmy is again aboard the ferry boat, able to see the man from the top deck. Standing there, still smiling. Comforting the lost souls. Still present as the South Tower collapses in a tidal wave of steel, dust and smoke.

The Angel of Death never moves. For this angel will never allow souls to feel lost.

"Open your eyes." Jimmy opens his eyes, instantly shaking his head. Working to process his experience. Quickly explaining the vision to Joe. The identity of the smiling man. The truth. And what he said to Jimmy. "How do you feel?" Joe's eyes a bit red themselves.

Jimmy stays quiet for a moment or two following the question. "A...awake. Does that even make sense? I don't know how else to describe it." Joe doesn't reply. Awake is enough.

Jimmy quickly interrupts the quiet. "I need to speak with him." What was once fear transforms into hardened determination. It's time for Jimmy to use his voice.

"Okay, then. Close your eyes. And awaken."

As his eyes close, Joe extends his left index finger and pushes ever so gently into Jimmy's forehead. Leaving a mild impression in the spot between his eyebrows. The heat and vibration of the stones provide the transport back in time. Again, placing him in the exact moment he wants to be.

Standing there, in the middle of the marina, time again stops. All movement around Jimmy and the Angel of Death ceasing. Their eyes locking again. The Angel of Death responds with his warm smile. Arms outstretched, hands open, palms facing upward.

"I would like to speak with you." Jimmy's words echo with conviction, absent of fear or anger.

"Please do. I'm here to help you as well. Are you feeling lost?" the Angel of Death's compassionate voice replies.

Both in his vision and seated on the bench, Jimmy straightens his spine, body and soul enmeshing as one. "Yes, I am."

"And why do you feel that way?"

"Was this day meant to be my last? Did I somehow cheat what was intended for me?"

The angelic smile widens. Emitting the glow and warmth of the morning's rays. "The answer you seek is not mine to provide. For your heart already holds the key. Be unafraid to open its treasure." Pausing momentarily. Jimmy responds, answering the Angel of Death, "*I believe I am meant to live.*" The sentence echoes with absolute faith. Truth. A joyful smile greets the words. "Indeed." The Angel of Death's head lowers in recognition of the answer. Then extending his right arm skyward, hand open. Motioning towards the ferry landing.

"Allow what has been lost to be found once again."

Empowered by hearing his own words and the comforting response from the Angel of Death, Jimmy turns towards the ferry. Confident it will be there, same as always. When he turns to leave, *to live*, a new sight appears. It isn't the ferry dock, the boat or the throngs of people awaiting rescue.

Jimmy is instead greeted by the single most stunning sunrise he's ever witnessed. Splendid rays of sunshine materializing in front of him in all their glory. The full spectrum of red, orange, pink, and yellow. A palette of spectacular colors all blending together in harmony over the deep blue horizon. Swirling seamlessly together, painted by a divine hand. Celestial light and warmth blanketing the landscape. "It's beautiful..." a whisper softly emerges on the park bench.

Within the image, Jimmy shields his eyes to manage the glare. Never before experiencing such a magnificent sight. The image calls him forward. The beginning of a new day. The darkness of the attacks behind him drifts away. Jimmy's focus now fully on what lies ahead. Promise. Possibility. All the beauty of life. He moves assuredly towards the glorious sunrise. Turning one final time, seeing the Angel of Death standing in the shadow of the Twin Towers.

Now comforting the living as well.

Jimmy bowing his head towards the Angel of Death. Overcome with gratitude and a sense of peace. The Angel of Death speaks again, softly. Despite the distance between them, Jimmy hears him clearly: "And live you shall."

"Are you ready to open your eyes?" Joe asks, observing the glowing smile adorning Jimmy's face. Jimmy's eyes remain closed. He draws in a deep, deep breath. Breathing in life anew. "Yes. Yes, I am." Jimmy's smile widening, mirroring that of the angel he just encountered.

Eyelids struggle to flicker open, having been closed with such an intense, driven focus on what lies within. As Jimmy's sight slowly returns to the park bench, the pending darkness of the evening is not visible before him. Rather, the world before him is aglow. Jimmy sees the glistening river of light in front of him. It is flowing all around him, encircling the two friends, the water, the trees and stretching well beyond the limits of mortal sight.

The wonder of the unseen.

Blink.

It's gone. Only a momentary glimpse, yet a profoundly ever-lasting moment in time.

Jimmy laughs, feeling as though he is afforded a gift that so few have the opportunity to experience. Continuing with several additional deep breaths. Inhaling the river of light into the wellspring of his heart, exhaling gratitude for those he's shared the path with today. The park appears to move slower as he continues the practice. The connections, the natural state of being, growing more present with each passing breath. Grass, trees, water, birds. Everything moving together in harmony. *Growing together.*

The splendor of the world he lives in matches the image held in Jimmy's mind, now also forever seated in his heart.

The day's sunset moves into its final stages behind the bridge. The shadows of the two men on the bench growing longer as dusk approaches. "Thank you, Joe."

"Again, kid. That one was all you."

Jimmy eagerly describes his experience to Joe. The encounter with the Angel of Death, the magnificent sunrise. What he finally said to the Angel of Death. The courageous words that were met with an angelic smile. "I believe I am meant to live." And the words that accompanied the loving smile in return: "And live you shall."

Jimmy laughs aloud.

Joe smiles, enjoying the blissful state. "What are you laughing at now, you silly goose?" He meets Jimmy's laugh with one of his own. "I can't wait to tell Quinn what it was like running into you today." Another burst of laughter follows. "Just remember, I didn't do anything. Only sat here and asked you to close your eyes. You made the choices on the path today."

"One question, though. Who was I meant to forgive?" Pausing, a knowing grin appears on Joe's face as he considers the answer, the setting sun enhancing its warmth.

"You. For living."

Jimmy's immense joy gives way to a greater release. The burden of guilt is lifted. An emotional dam breaks, setting forth a cascade of tears. Jimmy openly sobbing into the palms of his hands.

Joe quietly places his sturdy right hand on Jimmy's left shoulder as he hunches over. Letting him know he is not alone. Letting him know that he is never alone. After a few minutes, the flow of tears slows, calmly ceasing. *Jimmy finally forgives himself for living.*

In the space created by the grace and love of an open heart, a new feeling emerges. At least one that feels new again.

"How are you feeling now?" Joe quietly inquires. Wrinkling his brow, Jimmy has to find the word. Is there such a word to describe this feeling? Jimmy exudes a peaceful tone, "Free. Just...free." No judgment or penance or punishment accompany the release. The innocent shouldered a great burden far longer than ever intended.

"Free to do what?"

"Not what. Who." Jimmy replies.

"Well said, kid."

"Free to move towards that sunrise. Free to be who I am meant to be." Jimmy then repeats the words he spoke in his vision to the Angel of Death, "I believe I am meant to live."

"Indeed, you are. The real choice is how." Joe echoes the words and lessons of the angels.

Jimmy sits quietly, uncovering another truth from the day as Joe's words sow another seed. The truth about death. There to comfort. Ever-present in the darkest of moments in order to show us the beauty of living.

A Humble Guide

21

THE SUNSET NEARLY COMPLETE AS THE TWO FRIENDS
SIT TOGETHER ON THE PARK BENCH FACING THE
WATERWAY.

The park lights flicker as they begin the nightly ritual, stead-
fastly illuminating their surroundings. The water calming for
the night as well, no more container ships will pass through this
evening. The gentle lapping of waves from the steady current
providing the backdrop for the silence between the men. They
are alone, the last two patrons in the park today.

Jimmy slowly and gratefully hands the stones back to Joe.

Joe pauses and closes his eyes as he grips them with his
calloused right hand, as if absorbing the experience and the
energy himself. Then he simply places them back into their
leather pouch, tying the tiny little knot and returning the contents
back to his coat pocket.

"Joe, who are you? Really?" As genuine and thoughtful a
question ever asked by either of them.

"Who I am is a matter of perspective as well, isn't it?"

Jimmy is tired, but sensing the day coming to a close, embraces the banter. "More perspective, huh? I'm not exactly sure my body can handle much more at this point." Jimmy grins as he speaks. Eager for an answer, any answer, but within his heart, knowing perhaps one open point to return to would help ease their pending separation.

"Go ahead. Give it a shot. You'll be fine."

Jimmy pauses momentarily before answering. "I'd say you're a guide. Just like you mentioned when talking about the true measure of how we impact each other's lives. You saw a light in me and helped guide me to it. Thank you."

"It's an honor, kid. I accept guide and thank you for that. Remember, though, you chose this path. I am fortunate enough to have walked it with you." Joe places his right hand over his heart, as if to direct the words towards an intended location.

"Walked? Not walk?" Jimmy still a bit foggy from the experience with the stones, but clear enough to distinguish between the two words. "What do you mean 'walked'?"

"This time, it's my turn to head home," Joe states sincerely, a hint of sadness in his voice.

"Wait, what? You can't leave. Not now. What do I do next?"

"I would suggest you text Quinn to come and pick you up. This bench doesn't look like an appealing place to spend the night."

"You know what I mean."

"Remember. Not what, who." Joe continues. "Here. Take this. It's time for you to have it." Reaching out his right hand and offering the tattered leather book to Jimmy. "No! I can't. That's yours. You've been reading it for as long as I've known you! You *have* to keep it!"

"No, I don't. It's yours now."

"Why? Is this it? Is this the end?"

"That depends on perspective, too, doesn't it?" Still guiding.

Jimmy reaches for a sign that he still needs Joe. But under a different lens, perhaps Joe is right. Again. It's time. And this isn't the end.

Succumbing to the realization, Jimmy speaks reverently. "I understand. Thank you for today, for all the days on this path, for everything. But I'm still not sure about the book. That's always something you've carried."

"Now, I will always carry today with me. And, hopefully, you will learn what I did about this book."

"What's that?"

"I believe that answer will come at the right time."

Joe then stands up slowly from the bench. Rubbing his neck, twisting his torso and rolling his ankles. The day's journey, while not far measured in distance, exacting a toll on him as well. "Now give ol' 'Carpenter Joe' a hug. Even though I'm still not that old, you know."

"I know. At least not as old as you're going to be." Jimmy stands slowly himself. Still gaining his equilibrium from his experience seated on the park bench. Reality and perspective aligning themselves.

Once stable, the men embrace each other. All of the power, love and emotion of today, of a lifetime together, combine forces in the moment. It's the type of hug you remember forever. Always longing to replicate it, knowing how rare such embraces are. Each man allows for a few tears. Joy and sadness mixing together one final time.

Joe the first to speak, holding onto Jimmy's shoulders as he does.

"Now that you know your path, follow it. It is designed for you. And know that no matter where the path leads, *you never walk alone*." Jimmy's eyes water, unsure if there are any tears left to shed. His lips pursing with understanding and determination.

I know who I am.

Joe lets go of Jimmy. The men now free to choose their own path home. Joe turns and takes a path to the left, the one that leads its way out of the park, passing under the bridge soaring above. Towards the setting sun.

Jimmy chooses to walk right, book in his left hand cradled against his hip. Just like his guide.

Texting Quinn to confirm the pick-up spot. She would be there in ten minutes or so. Happy to hear from him, it's been awhile, and she begun to worry. "Nothing to worry about," the text back reads. "See you soon beautiful."

Several yards into his way out of the park, Jimmy stops. He turns and glimpses back at Joe, himself nearing the exit of the park. Finally, Joe is on his way home. "Thanks again Joe. Thank you for always being there for me."

Just then, Joe stops, sensing one more opportunity to serve as a guide on this path. Turning, seeing Jimmy standing in the distance, looking back at him. Speaking aloud so that perhaps the vibrations of his words will find Jimmy.

"No. Thank you, son. Now you're free to follow your path. To live."

What's Inside

22

JIMMY ARRIVES AT THE DESIGNATED PICK-UP SPOT NEAR THE PONY LEAGUE FIELD BY MOM'S OLD HOUSE, PAUSING UNDER A STREETLIGHT. CLUTCHING JOE'S BOOK, CAUTIOUSLY OPENING THE SOFT LEATHER COVER, WORN THIN FROM YEARS OF USE BY ITS PREVIOUS OWNER.

After all this time, finally able to see what is in inside. And what he finds inside absolutely astonishes him. Even after a day filled with amazement.

Written inside the cover is a handwritten note addressed to Jimmy.

How? When?

Dear Kid,

I'm glad you're finally reading this. I've wanted, and waited, for so long to give you this book. Just know since you are holding it now, it's the right time. Gifts appear in our lives exactly when they are supposed to. They are loving reminders that all of life's teachings are meant for you. This book is no different.

Remember, the true measure of our lives is not by how brightly we shine our own light; rather, it is found in our openness to see the light in others and in guiding them so they, too, may shine brightly. It is my hope that in some small measure, I've guided your light. Just as you have profoundly guided mine.

You chose the road less traveled. And as the poem says, that has made all the difference. Not just for you, but also for your family, and all the lives you will encounter on the journey you are destined for.

As you walk your path, keep the thoughts in your heart on the orchard. Embrace life's lessons and the uncertainty that accompanies each choice. Allow room for forgiveness, including for yourself. And remember that grace and love are powerful allies, able to overcome darkness to reveal the truth. For there is profound beauty on the other side of darkness.

As you follow the path laid before you, regardless of its contours, you will surely never walk alone.

The book you now hold, like many others throughout time, is comprised of stories conveying perseverance, wisdom and courage. However, I believe you will come to see, as did I, those tales pale in comparison to what lies inside the most powerful and beautiful of all creations – the heart and soul of the reader.

An eternity of gratitude for being your guide,
Joe

Gently closing the cover of the book, Jimmy cradles it again in his left hand, hugging his hip. A wide smile across his face. "Thanks for showing me the way, Joe. I won't forget it."

Quinn pulls the black Jeep to the curb a few moments later. Greeting Jimmy with the same loving smile as when they last saw each other earlier in the day. That legendary smile. "Hey, sorry. You know it takes *for-e-ver* to say goodbye to everyone," she says apologetically.

"No worries. How is everyone? You mind driving, though?" Jimmy climbs into the passenger side.

Quinn immediately recognizes something is different. Calmer. Content. Jimmy is carrying a book for one thing. "Sure, I'll drive. Is everything okay? How was your day?" Quinn keenly interested in what the answer might be.

"I'm good. I'm finally…good."

Perhaps *someone* is different.

Peace permeates the car. Engulfing them both. "I'm glad to hear that. Would you want to tell me about your day? We have a long ride home together."

"Absolutely, I have a story to share. But let's hug those kiddos first, shall we? I'm feeling some giant dad hugs coming their way. One for each of them."

"Sounds like a plan to me. It's been a long day. So, Mama hugs go first!" Quinn also weary from an emotional day.

"Ha. Deal. I'm glad we made the trip, though." Jimmy rubbing his eyes, still red from his time in the park. "Me too. It's good we were there today. I think everyone appreciated it." Quinn continues, "So, um, what's the story all about? Maybe a little preview for me?"

"Not what. Who." Jimmy smiles as the words come out. A gentle laugh accompanying them. Told you I wouldn't forget, Joe.

It's night time on the drive home. Darkness covers the urban landscape, although Jimmy views it differently now. Because a new day would begin soon. The sunrise will come soon enough. For now, though, the brilliant perfection of the stars in the night sky are a sight to behold. In the meantime, a new life already begun. And with it, a new perspective.

The old Jeep turns onto the New Jersey Turnpike bridge leaving Bayonne, the road home ahead. In the distance, Jimmy sees the skyline of Lower Manhattan. "Hey Quinn." Unconsciously, she lowers the volume on the radio, Zac Brown Band's "From Now On" becoming background music for the couple. "Yeah, what's up? You're being awfully quiet."

"I think I can help people."

Quinn reflexively counters, "I don't think you can." Jimmy is mildly crushed by the response given the day's affairs. She then smiles softly as her next observation meets the air:

"I think you're *meant* to.*"

"Thank you." The sincerity of Jimmy's response lands firmly in Quinn's heart. Something *is* different. Is it new? Or maybe old? That depends on perspective, doesn't it? His mind drifts, eyes gazing out the passenger side window. A new skyline emerging in the years following September 11th. Contemporary soaring castles of steel and glass hopefully inspiring a new generation of kids from the old neighborhood.

Jimmy sits quietly thinking to himself as he peers through the passenger side window into the night sky. In the distance, One World Trade Center, the new beacon of Lower Manhattan, shines brightest amongst the glittering skyline.

That's where angels live.

"Let's go home, beautiful." Jimmy reaches over the console, grasping Quinn's hand, interlocking their fingers. It will be a breathtaking ride home.